W9-AGT-221

ADVANCE PRAISE FOR
The Passion and the Cross

"Especially in the Jubilee 'Year of Mercy' called by Pope Francis, you simply won't do any better than reading Rolheiser on *The Passion and the Cross*. Don't just read this book—savor it, pray with it, and return to it throughout the year."

—John L. Allen, Jr., associate editor, *Crux/Boston Globe*

"Ron Rolheiser wades into the Friday–Sunday mystery of faith with courage and honesty. He brings to his exposition his deep spirituality and that of the church. He lines out that spirituality with an acute pastoral sensibility. But at bottom his book is a witness to the transformative, scandalous truth of the Gospel whereby we are saved in the drama of God's love. Rolheiser is unflinching in his grasp of the hard, wondrous reality of God's presence in the person of Christ. Readers will find here compelling testimony to the recurring power of Easter in the daily living of our lives."

—Walter Brueggemann, Columbia Theological Seminary

"One of the greatest Christian spiritual writers of our age turns his gaze toward the mystery of suffering and the meaning of the cross. This profound and compassionate spiritual meditation will be of inestimable use to anyone who has ever suffered or struggled in life—which is to say, everyone."

—James Martin, S.J., author, *Jesus: A Pilgrimage*

"From this most trusted spiritual guide, one is invited to plumb the depths of mystery, entering into life's most challenging questions about suffering, death, life, hope, faith, and ultimate meaning. The answers lie in the cross. And while its secret cannot be totally comprehended, one learns from Rolheiser how it can be lived with both head and heart."

—Barbara E. Reid, O..P, vice president and academic dean,
professor of New Testament studies,
Catholic Theological Union

"If you think this is a predictable and usual commentary on the passion accounts of Jesus, be ready for a very grateful surprise! Here you will find years of reflection, prayer, and a life in deep union with the mystery of death, suffering, and the resurrection that comes with it. The course of Jesus's journey is the course of fulfilled humanity, and it seems to surely be the course of Rolheiser's journey."

—Richard Rohr, O.F.M., author, *Eager to Love*

"With his elegant prose and thought provoking imagery, Rolheiser brilliantly explores the mystery at the heart of the Christian faith. *The Passion and the Cross* challenges readers to enter more deeply into questions of faith, life, love, and suffering, and then offers the spiritual tools needed for the journey."

—Kerry Weber, managing editor, *America*,
author, *Mercy in the City*

THE PASSION AND THE CROSS

THE PASSION AND THE CROSS

RONALD ROLHEISER

Franciscan
MEDIA
Cincinnati, Ohio

Cover design by John Lucas
Cover image © Masterfile
Book design by Mark Sullivan

ISBN 978-1-61636-812-8
Copyright ©2015, Ronald Rolheiser. All rights reserved.

Published by Franciscan Media
28 W. Liberty St.
Cincinnati, OH 45202
www.FranciscanMedia.org

Printed in the United States of America.
Printed on acid-free paper.
15 16 17 18 19   5 4 3 2 1

CONTENTS

PREFACE

In the Gospels, Jesus tells us that there exists a certain secret, a hidden wisdom, which, should we grasp it, is the key to unraveling all the deep secrets of life. Conversely, should we miss it, we will never really understand life. However, for Jesus that secret is not some exotic, gnostic, or hidden code, accessible only to intellectual elites or certain religious cults. For Jesus, the hidden secret that holds the key to everything is the cross: the wisdom of the cross and the brokenness of the one who died on the cross. If we grasp that reality, we will have the key to understanding the rest of life; if we do not grasp that wisdom, the meaning of life will always be somewhat of a riddle to us.

What is the wisdom that is revealed in the cross? It is something that we generally grasp more existentially than intellectually. We know it in a dark, inchoate way. For example, we know what it means when we say: *We all have our crosses to bear.* We cannot ever explain that adequately but, at some intuitive level, we sense that our own sufferings connect to the sufferings of Jesus on the cross. Moreover, we do not just sense that our sufferings are somehow connected to the cross; we also sense that, like Jesus's sufferings, ours, too, are somehow redemptive. At some deep level we sense that suffering is working to mature us, to make us grow up, to make us more compassionate, and is opening us up more to hear the voice of God and the voices of others. In most of what we suffer in life, we sense that, despite the pain and heartbreak, there is meaning inside the suffering.

But that is more of an intuitive gut-feeling than an explanation. How do we understand this more fully intellectually? The answer is extremely complex and partly mystery. The great mysteries of life—God, love, faith, suffering, redemption—are always partly beyond us. There can be no full intellectual understanding of them precisely because they are bigger than our finite minds and hearts. Thank goodness. If we could fully grasp them, then they would be finite like us, and just as limited. But their wells are much deeper than our own.

What is the hidden wisdom inside the cross of Jesus? How does our brokenness connect to the brokenness of the one who died on the cross? How does carrying our own crosses help those around us? How does the death of Jesus on the cross wash us free of our sins? What are we saying to ourselves and others when we wear crosses around our necks or display them in our homes? And, very importantly, how do we accept the challenge to make the death of Jesus on the cross an example that we follow in our own lives? Trying to shed light on these questions is the task of this book.

A colleague of mine is fond of saying: "God, as I understand him, is not very well understood!" The cross of Christ, as we understand it, also is not very well understood. But it is felt, deeply, in the marrow of our bones and in the depths of our hearts as the deepest of all secrets.

Ronald Rolheiser

San Antonio, Texas

September 2, 2015

CHAPTER ONE

The Passion and the Garden of Gethsemane

THE PASSION AS THE GIFT OF JESUS'S PASSIVITY

W E SPEAK OF ONE SECTION of the Gospels, that which narrates Jesus's life from the Last Supper until his death and burial, as chronicling his "passion." On Good Friday, the lector begins the Gospel reading with the words: "The Passion of Our Lord Jesus Christ According to John."

Why do we call Jesus's suffering just before his death his passion?

Generally, this is not properly understood. We tend to think that *passion* here refers to intense sufferings, as in "passionate suffering." This is not wrong, but it misses a key point. Passion comes from the Latin *passio* meaning passiveness, non-activity, absorbing something more than actively doing anything. The "passion" of Jesus refers to that time in his life where his meaning for us is not defined by what he was doing but rather by what was being done to him. What is being said here?

The public life and ministry of Jesus can be divided into two distinct parts: Scholars estimate that Jesus spent about three years preaching and teaching before being put to death. For most of that time—in fact, for all of it except the last day—he was very much the doer:

in command, the active one, teaching, healing, performing miracles, giving counsel, eating with sinners, debating with church authorities, and generally, by activities of every sort, inviting his contemporaries into the life of God. And he was busy. He is described at times as being so pressured by people that he didn't even have time to eat. For almost all of his public life Jesus was actively doing something.

However, from the moment he walks out of the Last Supper room and begins to pray in Gethsemane, all that activity stops. He is no longer the one who is doing things for others, but the one who is having things done to him. In the garden, they arrest him, bind his hands, lead him to the high priest, then take him to Pilate. He is beaten, humiliated, stripped of his clothes, and eventually nailed to a cross where he dies. This constitutes his "passion," that time in his life and ministry where he ceases to be the doer and becomes the one who has things done to him.

What is so remarkable about this is that our faith teaches us that we are saved more through Jesus's passion (his death and suffering) than through all of his activity of preaching and doing miracles. How does this work?

Allow me an illustration: Ten years ago, my sister, Helen, an Ursuline nun, died of cancer. A nun for more than thirty years, she much loved her vocation and was much loved within it. For most of those thirty years, she served as a den mother to hundreds of young women who attended an academy run by her order. She loved those young women and was for them a mother, an older sister, and a mentor. For the last twenty years of her life, after our own mother died, she also served in that same capacity for our family, organizing us and keeping us together. Through all those years she was the active one, the consummate doer, the one that others expected to take charge. She relished the role. She loved doing things for others.

Nine months before she died, cancer struck her brutally, and she spent the last months of her life bedridden. Now things needed to be done for her and to her. Doctors, nurses, her sisters in community, and others took turns taking care of her. And, like Jesus from the time of his arrest until the moment of his death, her body too was humiliated, led around by others, stripped, prodded, and stared at by curious passersby. Indeed, like Jesus, she died thirsty, with a sponge held to her lips by someone else.

This was her passion. She, the one who had spent so many years doing things for others, now had to submit to having things done to her. But—and this is the point—like Jesus, she was able in that period of her life, when she was helpless and no longer in charge, to give life and meaning to others in a deeper way than she could when she was active and doing so many things for others.

There's a great lesson in this, not the least of which is how we view the terminally ill, the severely handicapped, and the sick. There's a lesson too on how we might understand ourselves when we are ill, helpless, and in need of care from others.

The cross teaches us that we, like Jesus, give as much to others in our passivities as in our activities. When we are no longer in charge, when we are beaten down by whatever—humiliated, suffering, and unable even to make ourselves understood by our loved ones—then we are undergoing our own passion and, like Jesus in his passion, have in that the opportunity to give our love and ourselves to others in a very deep way.

A Lover's Pain

The passion of Jesus, as we just saw, refers to the helplessness he had to endure during the last hours of his life, a helplessness extremely fruitful for him and for us.

And the first component of that helplessness is apparent in the Garden of Gethsemane, immediately after he celebrated the Last Supper. The Scriptures tell us that he went out into the garden with his disciples to pray for the strength he needed to face the ordeal that was now imminent.

It's significant that this agony should take place in a garden. In archetypal literature, a garden is not a place to pick cucumbers and onions. Archetypally, a garden is the place of delight, the place of love, the place to drink wine, the place where lovers meet in the moonlight, the place of intimacy. The garden is paradise. That's why Adam and Eve in their paradisiacal state are described as being in a garden.

So it's no accident that Jesus ends up having to sweat blood in a garden. And it's precisely as a lover that he's in agony there. The Jesus who sweats blood in the Garden of Gethsemane is not the great king, full of pain because the sheep will not heed the shepherd; nor is he the great magus, full of sorrow because nobody wants to pick up on the truth he's revealed; nor is he the great warrior, frustrated in his efforts to defeat the powers of sin, death, and darkness. These pains and frustrations mostly take place elsewhere, among the crowds, in the Temple, in the desert. The garden is for lovers: not for kings, magi, and warriors.

It is Jesus the lover—the one who calls us to intimacy and delight with him—who sweats blood in the garden. That's why, in describing his suffering during his passion, the evangelists do not focus on his physical sufferings. Indeed, Mark puts it all in a single line: "They led him out to crucify him" (Mark 15:20). What the Gospel writers focus on is not the scourging, the whips, the ropes, the nails, the physical pain—none of that. Rather, they emphasize that in all of this Jesus is alone, misunderstood, lonely, isolated, without support. What's emphasized is his suffering as a lover: the agony of a heart that is ultrasensitive, gentle, loving, understanding, warm, inviting, hungry to embrace everyone; but which instead finds itself misunderstood, alone, isolated, hated, brutalized, facing murder.

That's the point that too often has been missed in both spirituality and popular devotion. I remember as a young boy being instructed by a wonderful nun who told us that Jesus sweated blood in the Garden of Gethsemane because, in his divine nature, he was saddened when he foresaw that many people would not accept the sacrifice of his death. That's a wonderfully pious thought, but it misses the point of what happened in Gethsemane.

In Gethsemane, we see Jesus suffering as a lover. His agony is not that of the son of God, frustrated because many people will not accept his sacrifice; nor even the all-too-understandable fear of the physical pain that awaits him. No; his real pain is that of the lover who's been misunderstood and rejected in a way that is mortal and humiliating. What Jesus is undergoing in Gethsemane might aptly be paralleled to what a good, faithful, loving, very sensitive, and deeply respectful man or woman would feel if he or she were falsely accused of pedophilia, publicly judged as guilty, and then made to stand powerless, isolated, misunderstood, and falsely judged before the world, family, friends, and loved ones. Such a person would surely pray too: "If it is possible, let this cup pass from me!" (Matthew 26:39).

The agony in the garden is many things, but, first of all, it's Jesus's entry into the darkest black hole of human existence, the black hole of bitter misunderstanding, rejection, aloneness, loneliness, humiliation, and the helplessness to do anything about it. The agony in the garden is the black hole of sensitivity brutalized by callousness, love brutalized by hatred, goodness brutalized by misunderstanding, innocence brutalized by wrong judgment, forgiveness brutalized by murder, and heaven brutalized by hell. This is the deepest black hole of loneliness and it brings the lover inside us to the ground in agony, begging for release.

But, whenever our mouths are pushed into the dust of misunderstanding and loneliness inside that black hole, it's helpful to know that Jesus was there before us, tasting just our kind of loneliness.

A Lover's Drama

Several years ago, Mel Gibson produced and directed a movie which enjoyed a spectacular popularity. Entitled *The Passion of the Christ*, the movie depicts Jesus's paschal journey from the Garden of Gethsemane to his death on Golgotha, but with a very heavy emphasis on his physical suffering. The movie shows in graphic detail what someone who was being crucified might have had to endure in terms of being physically beaten, tortured, and humiliated.

While most church groups applauded the film and suggested that, finally, someone had made a movie that truly depicted Jesus's suffering, many Scripture scholars and spiritual writers were critical of the movie. Why? What's wrong with showing, at length and in graphic detail, the blood and gore of the crucifixion which, indeed, must have been pretty horrific?

What's wrong (or better yet, *amiss*) is that this is precisely what the Gospel accounts of Jesus's death *don't* do. As we saw, all four Gospels take pains to *not* focus on the physical sufferings of Jesus. Their descriptions of his physical sufferings are stunningly brief: "And with him they crucified two bandits" (Mark 15:27). "After flogging Jesus, [Pilate] handed him over to be crucified" (Mark 15:15). Why the brevity here? Why no detailed description?

The evangelists don't focus us on what Jesus endured physically because they want us to focus on something else, namely, on what

Jesus endured emotionally and morally. The passion of Jesus is, in its real depth, a moral drama, not a physical one; the suffering of a lover, not that of an athlete.

Thus we see that when Jesus is anticipating his passion, the anxiety he expresses is not about the whips that will lash him or the nails that will pierce his hands. Rather, he is pained and anxious about the aloneness he is facing, about how he will be betrayed and abandoned by those who profess to love him, and about how he will be, in the wonderful phraseology of the author and theologian Gil Bailie, "unanimity-minus-one."

That the passion of Jesus is a love-drama is also evident in its setting. It begins with his sweating blood in a garden, and ends with his being buried in a garden. This is significant because in archetypal symbolism, as we saw, gardens are not for growing vegetables or even for growing flowers. Gardens are for lovers, the place to experience delight, the place to drink wine, the place where Adam and Eve were naked and didn't know it, the place where one makes love. And so the evangelists place the beginning and the end of Jesus's passion in a garden to emphasize that it is Jesus-as-lover who is undergoing this drama.

And what precisely is the drama? When Jesus is sweating blood in the garden and begging his Father to spare him having to "drink the cup," the real choice he is facing is not: Will I let myself die or will I invoke divine power and save my life? Rather the choice is: "How will die? Will I die angry, bitter, and unforgiving; or will I die with a warm, forgiving heart?"

Of course, we know how Jesus resolved this drama, how he chose forgiveness and died forgiving his executioners, and how, inside all that darkness, he remained solidly inside the message that he had preached his whole life; namely, that love, community, and forgiveness will ultimately triumph.

Moreover, what Jesus did in that great moral drama is something we're supposed to imitate rather than simply admire, because that drama is ultimately the drama of love within our own lives also, presenting itself to us in countless ways. That is: At the end of our lives, how will we die? Will our hearts be angry, clinging, unforgiving, and bitter at the unfairness of life? Or, will our hearts be forgiving, grateful, empathic, and warm, as was the heart of Jesus when he said to his Father "not my will but yours be done"? (Luke 22:42).

Moreover, this is not a one-time major choice we face at the hour of death; it is also a choice we face daily, many times daily. Countless times in our daily interactions with others—our families, our colleagues, our friends, and with society at large—we suffer moments of coldness, misunderstanding, unfairness, and positive violation. These moments range from the indifference of a family member to our enthusiasm, to a sarcastic comment intended to hurt us, to a gross unfairness in our workplace, to being the victim of a prejudice or abuse. Our kitchen tables, our workplaces, our meeting rooms, and the streets we share with others—all are places where we daily experience, in small and big ways, what Jesus felt in the Garden of Gethsemane: unanimity-minus-one. In that darkness, will we let go of our light? In the face of hatred, will we let go of love? That's the real and central drama of the passion of the Christ: not the ropes, whips, and nails.

The Agony of the Ultimate Athlete

Luke's account of Gethsemane says this of Jesus: "In his anguish [*agonia*] he prayed more earnestly" (Luke 22:44). The word *agonia* as it is used here doesn't just describe the intensity of Jesus's suffering; it especially describes his readying of himself for the painful task that waits. How?

At the time of Jesus, the word *agony* had a double sense: Beyond its more obvious meaning, it also referred to a particular readying that an athlete would do just before entering the arena or stadium. An athlete would ready himself (in those days the athlete normally was a he) for the contest by working up a certain sweat (agony) with the idea that this exercise and the lather it produced would concentrate and ready both his energies and his muscles for the rigors that lay ahead. No athlete wants to enter the contest unprepared.

The Gospel writers want us to have this same image of Jesus as he leaves the Garden of Gethsemane: His agony has brought about a certain emotional, physical, and spiritual lather so that he is now readied, a focused athlete, properly prepared to enter the battle. Moreover, because his strengthening brings a certain divine energy, he is indeed more ready than any athlete.

Gethsemane teaches us that to enter the spiritual arena, we too first must be properly warmed up. Cold muscles are a hazard here as well: We cannot walk from self-pampering to self-sacrifice, from living in fear to acting in courage, and from cringing before the unknown to taking the leap of faith, without first, like Jesus in Gethsemane, readying ourselves through a certain *agonia*, that is, without undergoing a painful sweat that comes from facing what will be asked of us if we continue to live the truth.

The Canadian author and activist Mary Jo Leddy once commented that in order to live in real courage we must die before we die. In any situation that is dominated by fear, she asserts, we need to be "living the resurrection" before we die. This means that choosing not to die is not always the same thing as choosing to live. We need to choose truth, integrity, and duty even if it means pain and death; otherwise the deep instinct for self-preservation will cause us always to be more concerned about our own safety and comfort than about anything else—and fear will dominate our lives forever.

In the Garden of Gethsemane, Jesus dies before he dies, and thereby readies himself for what awaits him. The next day, when Pilate threatens him with death, Jesus stands in a freedom and courage that can be understood only if we understand what happened to him in the garden. When Pilate says to him: "Don't you know that I have power over you, power to take your life or to save it?" Jesus answers: "You have no power over me whatsoever. Nobody takes my life; I give it over freely" (see John 19:10–11). In essence, Pilate is threatening a man who is already dead. No big threat. Jesus had already undergone the *agonia*. In great anguish he had given his life over freely the night before, and so he is ready for whatever awaits him.

We see something similar in Óscar Romero of El Salvador, martyred in 1980. When Romero was first named an archbishop, he was a good, sincere man, but also someone who lived in timidity and fear. However, as he met with the poor and let them baptize him with the truth, he began to experience a certain *agonia*, namely, it became clearer and clearer to him that he was on a collision course which would eventually force him to choose between backing away from the truth so as to save his own life or speaking the truth and being killed for it. Understandably, he began to sweat a certain blood—a certain spiritual and emotional lather began to warm his spiritual muscles. At one point, he realized that he had to speak the truth; in doing so, he assured his own death. But he had readied himself. He had already suffered his Gethsemane *agonia*, and he could now act with courage because he had already given his life away and thus no longer lived in the paralyzing fear that someone might take it from him.

Martin Luther King, in his memorable speech "I Have a Dream," says the same thing: Choosing self-preservation is not necessarily choosing life. Sometimes we need to accept opposition to choose community; sometimes we need to accept bitter pain to choose health; sometimes we need to accept a fearful free-fall to choose safety; and sometimes we need to accept death in order to choose life. If we let fear stop us from doing that, our lives will never be whole again.

We have nothing to fear but fear itself; easily said, but mostly our lives are dominated by it. We may be sincere and good, but we're also fearful—fearful of pain, of losing loved ones, of misunderstanding, of opposition, of sickness, of shame, of discomfort of all kinds and, ultimately, of death. Deep inside us is a powerful pressure to do whatever it takes to ensure our own lives, safety, and security.

And so it's not on the basis of nature that we give our lives away or move toward real courage. Like an athlete preparing for a tough contest, we must train for this. Like Jesus in the Garden of Gethsemane, we must die before we die; we must experience a courage-inducing *agonia*, so that, already having given it all away, we no longer live in the paralyzing fear that someone might take it from us.

The Hardest Thing of All

"When you carry someone's cross, don't send him or her the bill!"

This is one of the lessons of Gethsemane. The challenge of being an adult, one who helps carry life for others, is to give ourselves over in love, duty, and service without resentment. Those last words are key: Real love is not simply a matter of giving ourselves over in service and duty (mostly we have to do this anyway, whether we want to or not), it's a question of giving ourselves over without being resentful.

This was one of the struggles of Jesus in Gethsemane. He was asked to give up his life and freedom for something higher and, like all of us, felt a fierce resistance. Nobody, easily and naturally, gives himself or herself over to the deeper demands of love, duty, and service. Transformation through prayer is needed to bring us there.

We see this in Jesus: Only after having prayed is he finally able to say: "Yet, not my will but yours be done" (Luke 22:42). When he says this, his gift is pure. He is able to give himself over without resentment to the demands of a love which will take his whole life. After his prayer in Gethsemane, he is able to do what he needs to do without the feeling that he is a victim.

Jesus is victimized, but never a victim. When Pontius Pilate tries to intimidate him by telling him, "I can save your life or I can take it," Jesus responds: "Nobody takes my life from me; I give it up freely!" (see John 19:10–11). That translates to: "You can't take from me by force what I have already freely given over out of love!"

And that's the lesson: We become life-giving adults and our love becomes free of manipulation only when we can say this and mean it: *"Nobody takes my love and service from me; I give it over freely!"* Only when we stop seeing duty as an unfair burden that we haven't chosen can we love and serve others without resentment and without making others feel guilty because of what it's costing us.

But it's not easy to say those words and mean them. Like Jesus in the face of the deeper demands of love and duty, we initially say: *"Let this cup pass! There's got to be a way out of this, a way for me to become free of this."* That's natural. It's natural to want our freedom, to want to be free of burdens, of duty, of unfair circumstance. Nobody wants a martyrdom that he or she didn't sign up for!

But eventually this form of martyrdom finds us all. If we are sensitive and good-hearted, love will frequently become duty, demanding circumstance, and an invitation to sacrifice ourselves for someone or something else. Always there will be someone or something making demands on our freedom and opportunity: children who need us, an aging parent who has only us, family obligations, a spouse with an illness, a crisis at our workplace, a tsunami in Asia, a war we don't want, a church that needs volunteers—the obligations that come from being sensitive to the demands of God, family, church, country, morality, and the poor.

The world is not divided up between those who are burdened by duty and those who are free of it: Anyone who is sensitive and good is burdened by duty. Rather, the world is divided up between those who are burdened with duty and are resentful about it, and those who are burdened with duty and are not resentful about it.

That is very much the lesson of Gethsemane: What Jesus gave over to his Father in the garden is not perhaps so much his life, since his enemies were closing in on him and he might have had to die in any case, irrespective of any willingness or unwillingness on his part. Thousands of people die violently every day, against their will. There's nothing special in that. What's special in Jesus is how he prepared himself to meet that death, namely, by being willing to die without resentment, without putting a price tag on it, without making anyone feel guilty about it, and with a heart that was warm rather than cold, forgiving rather than bitter, and large and understanding enough that it didn't have to demand its due. In the face of bitter duty, he took his life and his love and made them a free gift.

That's the greatest struggle we have in love. We're good people, mostly. But, like the older brother in the parable of the Prodigal Son, all too often we nurse resentment, even as we do all the right things. That leaves us outside the house of love: hearing the music, but unable to dance and bitter about life's unfairness. At some point, we need to say, "Not my will, but yours, be done."

If we say these words and mean them, we will taste real freedom—maybe for the first time.

Undergoing Moral Loneliness

Our deepest loneliness is not sexual, but moral. More than we yearn for someone to sleep with sexually and emotionally, we yearn for someone to sleep with morally. What we really want is a soul mate.

What does this mean?

Ancient philosophers and mystics used to say that, before being born, each soul is kissed by God and then goes through life always, in some dark way, remembering that kiss and measuring everything in relation to its original sweetness.

Inside each of us, there is a dark memory of having once been touched and caressed by hands far gentler than our own. That caress has left a permanent imprint inside us, one so tender and good that its memory becomes a prism through which we see everything else.

Thus we recognize love and truth outside of us precisely because they resonate with something that is already *inside* us. Things "touch our hearts" because they awaken a memory of that original kiss. Moreover, because we have a memory of once having been perfectly touched, caressed, and loved, every experience we meet in life falls a little short. We have already had something deeper. When we feel frustrated, angry, betrayed, violated, or enraged it is because our outside experience does not honor what we already know and cling to inside.

And that dark memory of first love creates a place inside us where we hold all that is precious and sacred. It is the place we most guard from others, but the place where we would most want others to enter; the place where we are the most deeply alone and the place of intimacy; the place of innocence and the place where we are violated; the place of compassion and the place of rage.

The yearning and pain we feel here can be called moral loneliness because we are feeling lonely in that precise place where we feel most strongly about the right and wrong of things: that is, we feel alone in that place where all that is most precious to us is cherished, guarded, and feels vulnerable when it is not properly honored.

Paradoxically, it is the place where we most want someone to enter and yet where we are most guarded. On the one hand, we yearn to be touched inside this tender space because we already know the joy of being caressed there. On the other hand, we don't often or easily let anyone enter there. Why? Because what is most precious in us is also what is most vulnerable to violation and we are, and rightly so, deeply cautious about whom we admit to that sacred place. Thus, we often feel wrenchingly alone in our deepest center.

A fierce loneliness results; a moral aching. More deeply than we long for a sexual partner, we long for moral affinity, for someone to visit us in that deep part where all that is most precious is cherished and guarded. Our deepest longing is for a partner to sleep with morally—a kindred spirit, a soul mate. Great friendships and great marriages, invariably, have this at their root: deep moral affinity. The persons in these relationships are "lovers" in the truest sense because they sleep with each other at the deepest level, irrespective of whether they have sex or not. In terms of feeling, this kind of love is experienced as a "coming home," as finding a home, bone of my bone. Sometimes, though not always, it is accompanied by romantic love and sexual attraction. Always, however, there is a sense that the other is a kindred spirit, one whose affinity with you is founded upon valuing precisely the same things you do.

But such a love, as we know, is not easily found. Most of us spend our lives looking for it: searching, restless, dissatisfied, and morally lonely.

It's this kind of loneliness that brought Jesus to his knees in the Garden of Gethsemane. The blood he sweated there is the blood of a lover, the blood of one betrayed, morally betrayed, and hung out to dry.

Nikos Kazantzakis once wrote that virtue is lonely because, at the end of the day, it is jealous of vice. "Virtue," he writes, "sits on its lonely perch and weeps for all it's missed out on."[1] Not quite, though perhaps that's what it feels like.

But the pain of virtue, while not immune to jealousy, is a whole lot deeper than Kazantzakis (and conventional wisdom) suspect. It's the pain of Gethsemane, of moral loneliness, the ache of not having anyone to sleep with morally.

One of the lessons of Gethsemane is that when we sweat our moral aloneness (without giving in to compensation or bitterness) we undergo a moral alchemy that can produce a great nobility of soul. "What is madness," Theodore Roethke asks, "but nobility of soul at odds with circumstance?"[2] True. And that madness intensifies loneliness, even as, more than anything else, it opens the soul to the possibility of finally finding a kindred spirit.

Being Put to the Test

"A common soldier dies without fear, but Jesus died afraid."

Iris Murdoch wrote those words and they teach one of the lessons of Gethsemane. The Garden of Gethsemane is also the place where we are put to the test. What does this mean?

The great spiritual writer Henri Nouwen once wrote a book, *In Memoriam*, within which he tried to come to grips with his mother's death. The manner of her death had surprised him and left him struggling with some painful doubts and questions. Why?

His mother had lived a full life; she'd died surrounded by a loving family and friends, and in her final illness had been made as comfortable and pain-free as possible by the best of modern medicine. What's troubling about that?

She'd died struggling, it seemed, with her faith, unable to find at the most crucial moment of her life consolation from the God she'd loved and served so faithfully her whole life.

Henri's mother, as he explains at the beginning of the book, had been a woman of exceptional faith and goodness. He was teaching abroad when he received the phone call that she was dying. Flying home to be with her, he mused naively how, painful as it was going to be, his mother's death would be her final gift of herself and her faith to her family. A woman who had given them the faith during her life would surely deepen that gift by the way in which she would face her death.

But what he met in his mother and her struggles as she died was, at least to outward appearances, very different. Far from being peaceful and serene in her faith, she fought doubt and fear, struggling, it seemed, to continue to believe and trust what she had believed in and trusted in her whole life. For Henri, expecting that someone of such deep faith should die serenely and without fear, this was very disconcerting. *Why would God do this?* he asked. *Why would someone of such deep faith seemingly struggle so badly just before her death?*

The answer eventually came to him: All her life, his mother had prayed to be like Jesus and to die like Jesus. Shouldn't it make sense then that she should die like Jesus, struggling mightily with doubt and darkness, having to utter, "My God, my God, why have you forsaken me"? Jesus didn't die serenely, but struggling with doubt. Shouldn't his most committed followers expect a similar struggle?

The great mystics called this struggle "the dark night of faith;" an experience within which God purifies us by seemingly withdrawing all sense of his presence so that our thoughts and feelings run dry and we can no longer imagine God's existence. We become, in our hearts and heads, atheists at that moment, though something in our souls knows another reality.

It's an awful feeling, one of the worst pains possible. Darkness, chaos, and fear overwhelm us and we stand, literally, on the brink of nothingness, of nonexistence, sensing our finitude, littleness, and loneliness in a way we never sensed them before. We feel exactly what it would mean to live in a universe where there is no God.

The great doctors of the soul tell us that while nobody is immune from this trial, it is generally experienced in so radical a way only by those who are the most mature in the faith and thus more ready to be purified by its particular fire. It's not surprising then that it is experienced so strongly by people like Henri Nouwen's mother.

The rest of us tend to get it in bits and pieces. Little doses of what Jesus experienced on the cross appear in our lives, reveal the fearful edges of nothingness, and let us taste for a moment what reality would feel like if there were no God. Part of the darkness and pain of that (and why it feels as if we are suddenly atheists) is that, in that experience, we come to realize that our thoughts about God are not God and how we imagine faith is not faith. God is beyond what we can feel and imagine, and faith is not a warm feeling in the heart or a certainty in the mind, but a brand in the soul, beyond thought and feeling.

One way or the other, all of us have to learn this. But we'd like the lesson to come to us a bit more gently than how it came to Jesus in his last hours. Whenever we pray the Lord's Prayer and say, "Do not put us to the test," we're asking God to spare us from this night of doubt.

When Jesus walked into the Garden of Gethsemane, he told his disciples, "Pray not to be put to the test" (see Matthew 26:41). We need to pray for that because real faith can sometimes feel like doubt, and serenity can too easily turn into dark fear.

Sweating Blood

"In his anguish he prayed even more earnestly, and his sweat fell to the ground like great drops of blood."

Luke gives us this picture of Jesus in the Garden of Gethsemane (see Luke 22:44.) What's happening inside Jesus here?

Several years ago, there was a TV series entitled *Thirtysomething*. One of the episodes ran this way:

A group of men had gathered for a "men-only" party at a hotel. One of the men at the party, a married man, found himself attracted to one of the hotel managers, a young woman who was on duty that night, in charge of hospitality. He had to deal with her all evening in terms of making arrangements for food, drink, and music. She was attracted to him too, and as the evening went on their bond grew. Though nothing but practical conversation was exchanged, the romantic chemistry between them began to intensify. Each sensed it without, of course, revealing it to the other.

As the evening drew to a close, both did what comes naturally: They lingered near each other and found every kind of practical excuse to prolong their contact, without really knowing what to say to each other but sensing that there was a special connection that they were reluctant to break off.

Finally, it was time to part. The man stalled, thanking her one last time for what she'd done for the group. She, not wanting to lose the moment, took the risk and said to him, "I very much enjoyed meeting you. Would you like to get together again sometime?"

He, guiltily fingering his wedding ring and apologizing for not being more forthright, did what too few of us would have the honesty and courage to do. He sweated a little blood and then said to her, "I'm sorry, but I'm married. I need to go home to my wife."

My dad used to say to me, "Unless you can sweat blood sometimes, you will never keep a commitment, in marriage, in priesthood, or in anything else. That's what it takes to be faithful!"

In essence, at least in miniature, that was Jesus's agony in the garden. The blood he was sweating was the blood of emotional crucifixion, the price of being faithful in love.

To be faithful, to love beyond daydreams, sometimes requires—in hotel rooms, in gardens, at parties, in our workplaces, in places where wine is drunk, and in every place where people gather and intimacies are exchanged—that we enter a great loneliness, the loneliness of moral integrity, the loneliness of fidelity, the loneliness of duty, the loneliness of renouncing an overpowering desire, the loneliness of losing life so that we might find it in a higher way.

And that isn't easy. Jesus didn't find it easy and neither do we. What love and fidelity require will drive us to our knees in anguish sometimes, and, like Jesus in Gethsemane, we will find ourselves begging God for a means to still have our own way—to have our cake and eat it too, to find some way around fidelity, vow, promise, and duty.

This is a lover's anguish because the part in us that's agonizing and resisting is that part of the heart that stewards intimacy, romance, and embrace. The lover in us is having to let go of some very precious things; it's having to die to something for the sake of something else, and that's emotionally crucifying.

The account of Jesus sweating blood in the Garden of Gethsemane is, among other things, a powerful mystical image that tells us it's not enough simply to be sincere and follow the heart's desires. Sometimes love and fidelity demand that, like Jesus, in anguish and tears, we say to God, "Much as I desperately want this, I know I can't have it! Not my will, but yours, be done!"

A Stone's Throw Away from Everyone

Truth finds us in different ways. Sometimes we learn what something means not in a classroom, but in a hospital.

Several years ago, I was visiting a man dying of cancer in a hospital room. He was dying well, though nobody dies easy. He felt a deep loneliness, even as he was surrounded by people who loved him deeply. Here's how he described it: "I have a wonderful wife and children, and lots of family and friends. Someone is holding my hand almost every minute, but…I'm a stone's throw away from everyone. I'm dying and they're not. I'm inside of something into which they can't reach. It's awfully lonely, dying."

He had borrowed his salient phrase from Luke's Gospel where we are told that on the night before his death Jesus went to the Garden of Gethsemane with his disciples. There he invited them to pray with him as he struggled to find strength to face his death; but, as Luke cryptically adds, while he sweated blood, he was "a stone's throw away" from them (Luke 22:41).

How far is a stone's throw? It's distance enough to leave you in a place where no one can reach you. Just as we come out of the womb alone, we leave this earth alone. Jesus, like the man whom I just described, also faced his death knowing that he was loved by others, but also knowing that in the face of death he was entering a place where he was deeply and utterly alone.

This emphasis on aloneness is in fact one of the major points within the Passion narratives. In describing Jesus's death, perhaps more than anything else the Gospels want us to focus in on his aloneness, his abandonment, his being a stone's throw away from everyone. It is from within that utter aloneness that Jesus has to continue to give himself over in trust, love, forgiveness, and faith.

It's easy to believe in love when we feel loved; to forgive others when they are gracious toward us; and to believe in God when we feel strongly God's presence. The difficulty, the "test," comes when human love and divine consolation collapse, when we find ourselves surrounded by misunderstanding, abandonment, distrust, hatred, and doubt—especially at our loneliest hour, just at that moment when life itself is eclipsing. How do we respond then?

Will love, trust, forgiveness, and faith collapse in our hearts when the emotional pillars that normally sustain us collapse? Can we forgive someone who is hurting us when that person believes that we are the problem? Can we continue to love someone who hates us? Can we continue to believe in trust when everywhere around us we are experiencing betrayal? Can we let our hands and hearts be opened, stretched, and nailed to a cross even when we are fearful? Can we continue to have faith in God when every feeling inside us suggests God has abandoned us? Can we still hand over our spirit when we feel absolutely no human or divine support? Where are our hearts when we are "a stone's throw away" from everyone?

That, and not the capacity to physically endure scourging and nails, was the real test inside of Jesus's passion. Jesus's agony in the Garden was not so much an agonizing as to whether he would allow himself to be put to death or whether he would invoke divine power and escape. He recognized that he was going to die. The question for him was rather how he would die: Could he continue to surrender himself to a God and to a truth he had previously known when this now seemed to be belied by everything around him? Could he continue to trust? What kind of spirit would he hand over at the end? Would it be gracious or bitter? Forgiving or vengeful? Loving or hate-filled? Trusting or paranoid? Hope-filled or despairing?

That will be our test too in the end. One day each of us will also have to "give over" his or her spirit. On that day, will our hearts be warm or bitter?

And Seen from the Divine Side of Things

Each year on Good Friday the Passion of Jesus Christ According to John is read aloud in our churches. John's Gospel, as we know, was written later than the other Gospels, perhaps some seventy years after Jesus died, and those years gave John plenty of time to reflect upon Jesus's death and highlight a number of aspects that are not as evident in the other Gospels. What are those special aspects?

John's narrative of Jesus's death highlights his trial and the eventual judgment that he be put to death. But it is ingeniously written. John writes up the trial of Jesus in such a way that, while Jesus is the one being tried, *everyone else* is on trial except Jesus. Pilate is on trial, the Jewish authorities are on trial, Jesus's apostles and disciples are on trial, the crowds watching are on trial, and we who are hearing the story are on trial. Jesus alone is not on trial, even as his trial is judging everyone else. Hence, when Pilate asks Jesus: What is truth? Jesus's silence puts Pilate on trial by throwing Pilate back on his own silence: the truth of himself. It's the same for the rest of us.

Next, John emphasizes Jesus's divinity in his passion narrative. John's Gospel, as we know, highlights Jesus's preexistence with God and his divinity rather than his humanity. This shines through in his narrative. The Jesus being crucified in John's Gospel is always in control. He is unafraid, shows no weaknesses, carries his own cross, dies in serenity, and is buried like a king (with a staggering amount of myrrh and aloes, wrapped in cloths saturated with aromatic oils).

John's Jesus does not need any Simon of Cyrene to carry his cross, nor does he cry out in agony and abandonment. John writes up the Passion of Christ from the point of view of Jesus's divinity.

John then employs some powerful images to help score these points:

He has Judas and the soldiers arrive to arrest Jesus carrying "lanterns and torches." He intends strong irony here: Jesus is the light of the world and so the irony should not be missed in the fact that those opposing him come to him guiding themselves by artificial, flimsy lighting—lanterns and torches. This suggests, among other things, that they prefer darkness to light, and that they know that what they are doing can only be done at night because it would be shamefully exposed in the full light of day. The powers that oppose God need the cover of darkness and artificial light.

Next, at the end of the trial, Pilate brings Jesus out to the crowd and asks them whether or not they want to accept him as their king. They respond by saying, "We have no king but Caesar!" Historically, for a Jewish believer to say this at the time of Jesus would have been in effect a renunciation of his or her messianic hopes. That is true for us too: Every time we do not recognize the power of God in the one who is being crucified, we are renouncing our own messianic hope and admitting that the powers of this world are, for us, the deepest reality.

Further, John's Passion narrative emphasizes that Jesus was sentenced to death precisely at noon, the very hour on the eve of Passover when the Temple priests would begin to slaughter the paschal lambs. The inference is clear: Jesus is the real lamb who dies for sin.

Finally, in John's account of the Passion, after Jesus dies, soldiers come and pierce his side with a lance. Immediately blood and water flow out. This is a rich image: First of all, it symbolizes birth. When a baby is born, blood and water accompany the delivery. For John, Jesus's death is the birth of something new in our lives. What?

Christians have sometimes been too quick to take this image to infer the sacraments of baptism and Eucharist, with the outflow of blood symbolizing the Eucharist and the outflow of water symbolizing baptism. That may indeed be valid but there is, first, something more primal in that image: Blood symbolizes the flow of life inside us. Water both quenches thirst and washes dirt from our bodies. What John wants to say with this image is that those who witnessed the death of Jesus immediately recognized that the kind of love Jesus manifested in dying in this way created a new energy and freedom in their own lives. They felt both an energy and a cleansing, blood and water, flowing from Jesus's death. In essence, they felt a power flowing out of his death into their lives that allowed them to live with less fear, with less guilt, with more joy, and with more meaning. That is still true for us today.

John's Passion account puts us all on trial and renders a verdict that frees us from our deepest bondage.

CHAPTER TWO

The Cross as a Moral Revolution

The Most Revolutionary Moral Event in History

Among all the religious symbols in the world, none is more universal than the cross. You see crosses everywhere: on walls, on hillsides, in churches, in houses, in bedrooms, on chains around peoples' necks, on rings, on earrings, on old people, on young people, on believers, and on people who aren't sure what they believe. Not everyone can explain what the cross means or why they choose to wear one, but most everyone has an inchoate sense that it is a symbol—perhaps the ultimate symbol—of depth, love, fidelity, and faith.

And the cross is exactly that: the ultimate symbol of depth, love, fidelity, and faith. René Girard, the famed anthropologist, once commented that the cross of Jesus is "the single most revolutionary moral event in all of history." The world measures time by it. We are in the year 2015 (plus thirty-three years) since Jesus died on a cross and ever-increasing numbers of people began to organize their lives around its significance.

What is so morally revolutionary in the cross?

Precisely because it such a deep mystery, the cross is not easy to grasp intellectually. The deeper things in life, love, fidelity, morality, and faith are not mathematics, but mysteries whose unfathomable depths always leave room for still more to be understood. We never quite arrive at an adequate understanding of them.

But that doesn't mean that we don't know them. Knowing is different from understanding, and we intuit a lot more than we can intellectually imagine or express.

For example, *Time* magazine did a cover story some years ago on the meaning of the cross and interviewed a large number of people asking what the cross of Jesus meant to them. One woman admitted that she couldn't really explain what the cross of Jesus meant to her, but said that she had a sense of its meaning: When she was a young girl, her mother was murdered by a jealous boyfriend. When she saw the blood-soaked mattress and her mother's bloody handprint on the wall, she, right inside the horror and pain of the moment, knew in her gut, without being able to put words to it, that there was a deep and sacred connection between her mother's story (and her blood on that mattress) and Jesus's story (and his blood on the cross.) Sometimes the heart intuits where the head needs to go. In her deepest center she intuited the connection between her mother's blood and Jesus's blood, even though she couldn't articulate that connection in words. In street parlance, "she got it," without precisely understanding it.[3]

Beyond this gut-knowledge, what can we intellectually grasp about the meaning of the cross? What is its revolutionary moral character?

Much of what Jesus revealed to us is like a time-release medicine capsule. Throughout the centuries, slowly, gradually, incrementally, Jesus's message is dissolving more deeply into our consciousness. For example, Christianity is more than two thousand years old, but it took us nearly nineteen hundred years to fully grasp the fact that slavery is wrong, that it goes against heart of Jesus's teaching. The same can be said about the equality of women.

And this is particularly true about our understanding of the cross and what it teaches. For example: There have been popes for two thousand years, beginning with Peter, but it was only in our own generation that Pope John Paul II stood up and said with clarity that capital punishment shouldn't be imposed (independent of any arguments about whether or not it is a deterrent, brings closure to the victims' families or not, or can be argued in terms of justice). Capital punishment shouldn't be imposed because it goes against the heart of the Gospel as revealed in the cross; namely, that we should forgive murderers, not kill them.

That is just one of the morally revolutionary features inside of the cross. There are countless others. René Girard, speaking as an anthropologist, puts it one way when he says that the cross is the most revolutionary moral event in the history of the planet. Mark, the evangelist, speaking as a disciple of Jesus, puts it another way: For him, the cross of Jesus is the deep secret to everything.

In Mark's Gospel, to the extent that we understand the cross of Jesus, we grasp life's deepest secret. And the reverse is just as true: To the extent that we don't grasp the meaning of the cross, we miss the key that opens up life's deepest secrets. When we don't grasp the cross, life's deep mysteries become a riddle.

The Deep Secret to all Understanding

Everyone longs to know something that's secret, to know something that others don't know, but that you know, and the knowledge of which gives you some insight and advantage over others who are outside the inner circle of that secret. It has always been so. Historically this is called "gnosticism," which forever makes an appearance in one form or another.

Today we see this in society at large in the immense popularity of books like *The Da Vinci Code* and *The Celestine Prophecy*. Their lure is precisely in the hint that there are secrets that a few elite persons know that contain important, life-altering information of which we, the unenlightened, are ignorant. Our itch, of course, is to be inside these special circles. We see this paralleled sometimes in religious circles: in the over-fascination people have with the private revelations of various self-acclaimed mystics, in special books claiming to disclose critical new revelations from the Blessed Virgin Mary, and in the undue interest shown in things like the Third Secret of Fatima. Gnosticism has many cloaks.

At first glance, Jesus, in Mark's Gospel, seems to be hinting at just this sort of secret. He tells us there is a secret that is open to us which, if known, puts us into a special circle of enlightenment and community. In Mark 4:11, he tells his disciples, "To you has been given the secret of the kingdom of God, but for those outside, everything comes in parables." Clearly, here Jesus is distinguishing between two circles, one which grasps the secret and is then "inside," and the other which does not grasp the secret and is then "outside." Jesus seems to be saying that in following him we can be either "in" or "out," depending upon whether or not we grasp a certain secret. Genuine disciples are those who (in today's terminology) "get it," and those who "don't get it" remain outside. But what are we inside or outside of? More importantly, what is the secret?

For Jesus, the secret is the cross—that's the deep wisdom we need to grasp. If we understand the cross, all the rest of what Jesus teaches will make sense. Conversely, if we don't understand the cross, all the rest of what Jesus teaches won't make sense. Grasping the meaning of the cross is the secret to everything. But how, more concretely, should this be understood? What is the deep secret that lies inside the cross of Jesus? What, in essence, do we need to understand?

Various biblical commentators answer this in different, complementary ways. For some, it means grasping the wisdom that's revealed in the cross. For others, it means understanding the brokenness of Jesus on the cross. For still others, it means understanding the invitation that is inside the cross which beckons us to live out the demands of the cross. Each of these, in its own way, points to the most profound secret of all inside human understanding; namely, that in giving love away in total self-sacrifice, at the cost of humiliation, brokenness, and death, we ourselves come to what's deepest and fullest in life.

But, unlike all Gnostic secrets, ancient or contemporary, this is an open secret, available to everybody and, paradoxically, more accessible to the "little ones," the poor, and more hidden to "the wise and the clever." Jesus makes the point that he has no hidden secrets by emphasizing again and again that he speaks openly and in public, never in secret, but in synagogues and marketplaces. Jesus has no hidden secrets, only open secrets that we fail to grasp.

Interestingly, we see that in the Gospels, grasping the secret of the cross is not something we do once and for all. Sometimes we grasp it, and we are inside the circle of understanding; and sometimes we don't grasp it, and we are outside the circle of understanding. For example, after Peter denies Jesus during the passion, the Gospels tell us that "Peter went outside;" and they are referring to much more than simply stepping outside through some courtyard door. In denying that he knew Jesus and in not stepping forward to assume the weight of what would happen if he remained faithful, Peter was stepping outside the circle of both true discipleship and of a true understanding of life. His denial of Jesus took him "outside." We too, in our following of Jesus, sometimes step "outside" when we give in to temptation or adversity. But then, if we repent of our betrayal, like Peter, we can step back "inside."

There are various ways we can enter into an understanding of Jesus's message and try to appropriate it for our lives, but few, perhaps none, take us so immediately to the center as does the invitation from Jesus in the Gospel of Mark to grasp and accept the wisdom of the cross.

Trying to Understand a Mystery

The cross is an overrich symbol and a multivalent mystery. There are parts of its mystery that we can understand and parts of it that are beyond what our heads can grasp. It is also a very complex mystery, with multiple dimensions. How can we understand the cross? Theologians, classically, have tried to come to grips with the meaning of the cross (and of Jesus's death) by making a crucial distinction between what the cross has to teach us and how the cross saves us.

On the one hand, the cross of Jesus, as we will see shortly, is God's clearest revelation of what God is and how we are meant to live our lives in the face of that reality. The cross contains all of Jesus's teaching crystallized in one image, one powerful teaching. It says most powerfully what Jesus was trying to teach us during his whole active ministry. It is the ultimate revelation of God.

On the other hand, the cross of Jesus, as we will see later, is also God's ultimate saving act in this world. The cross is redemptive; it saves us. All Christians believe that somehow we are washed clean in the blood of Jesus, that Jesus is the Lamb of God who takes away the sins of the world, and that Jesus opened the gates of heaven for us. We are saved through the cross. It is also salvific.

Hence, one aid in understanding the cross of Jesus is to make a distinction between the cross as revelation and the cross as redemption. Neither of these concepts is easy to explain, though theologians do better with the first, the cross as revelation, than with the second, the cross as redemption.

We now look at each of these in turn.

CHAPTER THREE

The Cross as the Deepest Revelation of God

Tearing Away the "Curtain Veil"

There are so many haunting lines in the passion narratives. Who of us, for instance, is not stirred in the soul when the passion story is read in church and we come to the part where Jesus takes his last breath and there is that minute of silence when we all drop to our knees? No Good Friday homily is ever as effective as that single line ("he bowed his head and gave up his spirit") and the moving silence that ensues.

Another such line that has always haunted me is the one that follows immediately after Jesus dies and we are told that, at the very second of his death, "the veil of the temple was torn in two, from top to bottom." My imagination, even when I was very little, has always been able to picture that. I have this picture in my mind of it growing dark in the middle of the day and then at the second of Jesus's death, almost as if by lightning, the Temple veil is ripped from top to bottom while everyone looks on stunned, convinced now, too late, that the person they've just mocked and crucified is the Christ. It's a great picture. But, my imagination aside, what is really meant by that phrase that the veil of the Temple ripped open at the moment of Jesus's death?

Biblical scholars tell us that the veil of the Temple was precisely a curtain. It hid the "holy of holies." The ordinary worshipper in the Temple could not see what was behind it. It shielded a person from seeing into the holy. Thus, when the Gospel writers say that at the precise moment of Jesus's death the Temple veil was ripped apart from top to bottom, the point they are making is not, as my imagination would want it, that God shredded what was most precious to the those who crucified Jesus to show them how wrong they were. No. The point is rather a positive one.

The veil in the Temple physically separated the people from that part of the Temple that was "the holy of holies" and that was always beyond the sight of ordinary people. Only the priests, to do sacred ritual, went behind the curtain and saw what was there. What the Gospels are saying when they tell us that the death of Jesus ripped the Temple veil from top to bottom is that the cross of Jesus took away the veil that prevents us, the ordinary people, from seeing into the true "holy of holies," the inner heart of God. In Jesus's death we see right into the heart of God. There is no longer a veil between us and God's heart. The cross of Jesus shows us what God really looks like.

To understand the richness of this image, it is helpful to compare it to its parallel image in the Jewish Scriptures, namely, the image of the rainbow: The Scriptures tells us that God is "light," but, interestingly, we cannot see light. We see by light, but we don't see light itself, except in one instance—the rainbow. If light is shone through a prism, the prism refracts the light, literally breaking it up so that we see inside of it. And the result is stunning: We see that the inside of light is spectacularly beautiful, comprised of seven magnificent colors. In a rainbow, in one manner of speaking, we see the inside of God, physically, and we see that God's inside is beautiful.

The cross is a prism that refracts God's moral interior; it tears away the veil that prevents us from seeing inside God's heart, and what we see, like the colors in a rainbow, is spectacularly beautiful. The moral heart of God breaks down into spectacularly beautiful colors too: unconditional love and its various manifestations. The cross of Jesus is the real icon of the Trinity and it is also the ultimate revelation of God.

And what does it reveal? When we look into the heart of God, what do we see there?

Revealing Vulnerability as the Path to Intimacy

The cross of Jesus doesn't just reveal God as unconditional love; it also reveals how vulnerability is the path to intimacy. How is this revealed in the cross?

The best place to start is with God. What the cross tells us, more clearly than any other revelation, is that God is absolutely and utterly nonviolent and that God's vulnerability, which the cross invites us into, is a power for community with God and with each other. What's being said here? How does the cross reveal God as nonviolent?

We are forever connecting God to coercion, threat, guilt, reckoning, and to the idea that a power should somehow rise up and crush by force all that's evil. That concept is the main reason why so many of us either fear God, hate God, try to avoid God, or are disappointed in God ("Why doesn't God do something about the world?") But what Scripture reveals about God, and this is seen full-bloom on the cross, is that God is not coercion, threat, guilt, nor the great avenger of evil and sin.

Rather, God is love, light, truth, and beauty; a gentle if persistent invitation, one that's never a threat. God is like a mother, gently trying to coax another step out of a young child learning to walk ("Come on, try, just another step!") God exists as an infinite patience that endures all things; not as a great avenger, the hero in the movies, who kills all the bad guys when he has finally had enough. The cross of Christ reveals that God works far differently than do our movies and our imaginations. God never overpowers anyone.

Radically, of course, God could. God has all the power. However God's power to create love and community, paradoxically, works precisely by refusing to ever overpower. It works instead through vulnerability, through something the Gospels call *exousia*. What is this?

The Gospels tell us that when people witnessed Jesus's life and ministry they saw something that sharply differentiated him from others. He spoke with great power, unlike the Scribes and Pharisees. However they use a curious word to name that power. They never say that Jesus spoke with great energy or dynamism. Instead they use the Greek word, *exousia*, a word with no English equivalent, but whose meaning can be conveyed in an image:

If you would put the strongest man in the world into a room with a newborn baby, which of these two would be more powerful? Obviously, at one level, the man is more powerful—he could kill the baby if he wanted. But the baby possesses a different kind of power, a far deeper one, one that can move things muscles can't move. A baby has *exousia*; its vulnerability is a greater power. It doesn't need to out-muscle anyone. A baby invites and beckons; and all that's moral and deep in our conscience simply cannot walk away. It's no accident that God chose to be incarnated into this world as baby.

It's no accident either that Jesus died as he did on Good Friday. The cross reveals the power of God in this world, a power that is never the power of muscle, speed, brilliance, physical attractiveness, or a presence that leaves you no other choice but to acknowledge its superiority and bend your knee in obeisance. The world's power works this way, and movies end that way. But God's power is the power of *exousia*—a baby that lays helpless, muted, patient, beckoning for someone to take care of it. It's this power that lies at the deepest base of things and will, in the end, gently, have the final say. It's also the only power upon which love and community can be created because it, and it alone, ultimately softens rather than breaks the heart.

And it's a power that invites us in. It's good to know this so that we don't give in to bitterness and grow vicious ourselves when we are slighted and can't defend ourselves, when our dreams get crushed and there's nothing we can do about it, when we so desperately want to do something that stands out but haven't the talent to do so, or when we find ourselves a minority of one before a jeering crowd.

The cross of Christ tells us that at those moments of painful helplessness when we can't impress or overpower anyone, we are acting in a divine way, nonviolently, and in that vulnerability lies the secret to our coming to love and community.

Revealing God as Fellow-Sufferer and as Redeemer, not as Rescuer

Before you get serious about Jesus, first consider how good you are going to look on wood!

That's a quip from Daniel Berrigan rightly warning us that faith in Jesus and the resurrection won't save us from humiliation, pain, and death in this life. Faith isn't meant to do that. Jesus doesn't grant special exemptions to his friends, no more than God granted special exemptions to Jesus. We see this everywhere in the Gospels, though most clearly in Jesus's resurrection. To understand this, it's helpful to compare Jesus's resurrection to what Jesus himself does in raising Lazarus from the dead.

The Lazarus story raises a lot of questions. John, the evangelist, tells us the story: He begins by pointing out that Lazarus and his sisters, Martha and Mary, were very close friends of Jesus. Hence, we are understandably taken aback by Jesus's seeming lack of response to Lazarus's illness and the request to come and heal him. Here's the story:

Lazarus's sisters, Martha and Mary, sent word to Jesus that "the man you love is ill" with the implied request that Jesus should come and heal him. But Jesus's reaction is curious. He doesn't rush off immediately to try to heal his close friend. Instead he remains where he is for two days longer while his friend dies. Then, after Lazarus has died, he sets off to visit him. As he approaches the village where Lazarus has died, he is met by Martha and then, later, by Mary. Each, in turn, asks him the question: "Why?" Why, since you loved this man, did you not come to save him from death? Indeed, Mary's question implies even more: Why is it that God invariably seems absent when bad things happen to good people? Why doesn't God rescue his loved ones and save them from pain and death?

Jesus doesn't offer any theoretical apologia in response. Instead he asks where they have laid the body, lets them take him there, sees the burial site, weeps in sorrow, and then raises his dead friend back to life. So why did he let him die in the first place? The story raises the question: Why? Why didn't Jesus rush down to save Lazarus since he loved him?

The answer to that question teaches a very important lesson about Jesus, God, and faith—namely, that God is not a God who ordinarily rescues us, but rather is a God who redeems us. God doesn't ordinarily intervene to save us from humiliation, pain, and death; rather he redeems humiliation, pain, and death after the fact.

Simply put, Jesus treats Lazarus exactly the same way that God, the Father, treats Jesus: Jesus is deeply and intimately loved by his Father and yet his Father doesn't rescue him from humiliation, pain, and death. In his lowest hour, when he is humiliated, suffering, and dying on the cross, Jesus is jeered by the crowd with the challenge: "If God is your father, let him rescue you!" (Matthew 27:43). But there's no rescue. Instead Jesus dies inside the humiliation and pain. God raises him up only after his death.

This is one of the key revelations inside the cross: We have a redeeming, not a rescuing, God.

Indeed, the story of the raising of Lazarus in John's Gospel was meant to answer a burning question inside the first generation of Christians: They had known Jesus in the flesh, had been intimate friends with him, had seen him heal people and raise people from the dead, so why was he letting them die? Why wasn't Jesus rescuing them?

It took the early Christians some time to grasp that Jesus doesn't ordinarily give special exemptions to his friends, no more than God gave special exemptions to Jesus. So, like us, they struggled with the fact that someone can have a deep, genuine faith, be deeply loved by God, and still have to suffer humiliation, pain, and death like everyone else. God didn't spare Jesus from suffering and death, and Jesus doesn't spare us from them.

That is one of the key revelations inside of the cross and is the one we perhaps most misunderstand. We are forever predicating our faith on—and preaching—a rescuing God, a God who promises special exemptions to those of genuine faith. *Have a genuine faith in Jesus, and you will be spared from life's humiliations and pains! Have a genuine faith in Jesus, and prosperity will come your way! Believe in the resurrection, and rainbows will surround your life!*

Would it were so! But Jesus never promised us rescue, exemptions, immunity from cancer, or escape from death. Rather, he promised that, in the end, there will be redemption, vindication, immunity from suffering, and eternal life. But that's in the end; in the meantime, in the early and intermediate chapters of our lives, there will be the same kinds of humiliation, pain, and death that everyone else suffers.

The cross and resurrection of Jesus reveal a redeeming, not a rescuing, God.

Revealing God's Identification with the Victim and the Victim as Cornerstone

Some years ago, in Canada's prairies, not far from where I was born and raised, a man named Robert Latimer killed his severely handicapped daughter, Tracy. He put her into the family truck, hooked a tube to the exhaust, sealed the windows and doors, and let her fall asleep. He wasn't malicious in intent. He loved his daughter. In his mind, this was an act of mercy. He couldn't bear to see her suffer any longer. No one doubted his sincerity. His daughter was almost totally disabled physically and mentally, lived in constant pain, and there was no favorable prognosis in terms of her ever getting better or of her pain ever lessening. So he, in as humane a way as possible, ended her life.

Her death became a huge national story: a drawn-out court battle that lasted for years, ending up in the Supreme Court of Canada, and a countrywide moral and religious debate that bitterly divided families and communities. The death of this young girl, Tracy Latimer, raised an issue we can't agree on today: What's the value of a human life that is severely disabled?

What's the value of a life such as Tracy Latimer's? Biblically, the answer is clear: When someone is deemed expendable, for whatever reason, at that moment she or he becomes the most important person, spiritually, in the community: *"The stone that the builders rejected has become the cornerstone"* (Matthew 21:42). This means that the Tracy Latimers within our lives are a privileged place where the rest of us can experience God.

One of the central revelations of the cross is that there is a very privileged presence of God in the one who is excluded, in the one of whom society says: "Better that she should die for the people" (see John 11:50). Scripture is clear on this: Already in the Jewish Scriptures, we see that the prophets emphasize the idea that God has special sympathy for orphans, widows, and strangers. At that time, these particular groups had the least status, the least power, and were deemed the most expendable. They could be left to die so that society could get on with its more urgent business. The prophets' message was revolutionary: God has a special sympathy for those whom society deems least important, and how we treat those persons is the litmus test of our faith, morals, and religiosity.

Jesus takes this a notch further: In his teaching, not only does God have special sympathy for those whom society deems least important and most expendable, but God's very presence is identified with them: "Whatsoever you do to the least of these, you do to me!" (see Matthew 25:40). Jesus identifies God's presence with the outcasts, with the excluded ones, and he tells us that we have a privileged experience of God in our contact with them.

Nowhere is this stated more clearly than in Jesus's death on the cross: The crucified one is the stone rejected by the builders, the one deemed expendable so that normal life will not be disrupted. But the crucified one is also God and there is a special intimacy with God that can be had only in standing, as did Mary and John, near the cross, in solidarity with the crucified one, the one who is being excluded.

Sometimes that's hard to see and accept because, unlike Jesus, the excluded ones in our culture are not always innocent and loving. For example, the Oklahoma City bomber Timothy McVeigh was executed. Our society, like the high priest of old, had pronounced its judgment: "Better that one man should die for the people." But, unlike Jesus, Timothy McVeigh didn't radiate innocence, love, moral integrity, repentance, or most anything else that speaks of God's presence. So how is he the cornerstone for our building?

By his exclusion, by his being deemed expendable, by being the one executed. At the precise moment when his executioners spread his arms and lashed them to a table and the lethal injection was brought in, Timothy McVeigh became the Christ-figure: a man helplessly stretched out, unanimity-minus-one, better off dead for the benefit of others, grist for those who need a scapegoat, the focus for moral reflection, the central figure in the community, and the one who, for that moment and in that situation, becomes a privileged presence of God because, as the cross makes plain, God is specially present in the excluded one.

Many of us are familiar with an incident recorded by Elie Wiesel. In one of the Nazi death camps, a prisoner had escaped and, in retaliation, the Nazis took a young boy, hanged him publicly, and forced everyone to watch this horrific spectacle. As the young boy dangled on a rope in front of them, one man cursed bitterly, "Where is God now?" Another man answered, "There, on that rope. That's God!"

One of the revelations of the cross is precisely this: that in the crucified one, God is present.

Revealing our Invincible Ignorance

As Jesus is being crucified, he asks his Father to forgive his killers. "Father, forgive them; for they do not know what they are doing" (Luke 23:34).

Karl Rahner once made an interesting comment on this. He pointed out that, in fact, they did know. The people crucifying Jesus knew exactly what they were doing. They knew he was innocent, they knew their own jealousy, and they knew too that they were doing something wrong; just as we know, at least most of the time, when we are doing wrong. Our sense of right and wrong is not that easily derailed, even when we are caught up in a mob action where there is a certain moral blindness and safety in numbers.

So what does Jesus mean by this? What were his executioners ignorant of? How could they be innocent when they knew better? For Rahner, the statement, "they know not what they are doing," refers to something beyond conscious awareness. What those crucifying Jesus didn't know is how much they were loved. They weren't ignorant of their own motivation. They knew their own deceit. But they had too little knowledge and awareness of God's love for them. It's that ignorance that made them—and makes us—mostly innocent of real sin.

Scholastic thought used to distinguish between "culpable" and "inculpable" ignorance. It termed the latter "invincible ignorance" and defined it as a darkness, a lack of understanding, for which we are not responsible. In this framework of thought, you are not considered to be committing a sin when you do something wrong if you do it out of an ignorance that isn't your fault. For the Scholastics, in order to sin, you first have to have a certain awareness. Of what? Of love. Allow me an illustration:

Some years ago, I received a letter from a woman in her late forties. She began the letter by telling me that she could, in all truth, say that for the first forty years of her life she had not committed a sin.

Her words: "I grew up in a terrible home and was abused and unloved as child. I became bitter, suicidal, and acted out in every way.

I bit in order not to be bitten and broke every commandment except murder (which in fact I contemplated), but I really don't believe I ever sinned, even though I knew I was doing wrong at the time. Why don't I think I sinned? Because sin is a betrayal of love and nobody, as far as I knew, had ever loved me. God was loving me, I know that now, but I had no way of knowing or believing that then. I did what I needed to do to survive.

"Sometime after my fortieth birthday a miracle happened. I fell in love and that person fell in love with me. I experienced love for the first time. I know now what it means to sin because I'm loved. Now when I do something wrong, it is a sin because I am betraying love. But you first need to be loved in order to betray that. When I didn't know love and had no way of sensing God's love for me, I had nothing to betray, at least as far as I knew. That's why I believe that, even though I did many wrong things, I didn't sin."

Sin is a betrayal of love. However, you first have to be loved and, however dimly, sense that love before you can betray it. In Rahner's view, this is what lies behind Jesus's plea to his Father to forgive his killers because they don't know any better. On one level, of course, they do; but on another level, a far more important one, they don't. Like the woman whose letter I just quoted, they don't know how much they are loved. They are biting others in order not to be bitten.

There's more jealousy, hatred, anger, murder, adultery, slander, lying, and blasphemy at God in our world than there is sin. We're not so much bad as ignorant, inculpably so. Oftentimes when we do wrong, we aren't betraying love because we don't know love to begin with. That doesn't mean our behavior isn't destructive, that it doesn't ruin lives, wreak havoc with happiness, and that it doesn't continue (as Scripture so graphically puts it) to murder God out of ignorance. Our actions have real and often permanent effects. Those effects may never be trivialized. When we do wrong, we hurt others and hurt ourselves, even if we aren't sinning. Darkness is always the enemy of light. It's just that, more often than not I suspect, our actions may be wrong, very wrong, but they're not sinful because we don't know what we're doing. Our darkness is invincible, inculpable, something for which we aren't really fully responsible.

Mercifully, God's compassion and understanding are deeper than our own, and God's love can descend into hell itself and, even there, forgive and redeem us.

Revealing God's Power to "Descend into Hell"

There's a curious line in our creed which says that, immediately following his death, Jesus "descended into hell." What, possibly, can that mean?

Within the popular Christian mind-set we have the conception that, as a consequence of original sin, the gates of heaven were closed so that, from the time of Adam and Eve until the moment of Jesus's death, nobody could enter paradise. Only a divine act of reparation could again give human beings access to heaven, and that act of reparation was Jesus's death which "paid the debt of sin" and so opened the gates of heaven.

In this view of things, all the just who had died from the time of Adam and Eve until Jesus's death were asleep somewhere, in a Hades of sorts. Immediately following his death, Jesus descends to that underworld and awakens these souls and then triumphantly leads them into paradise. That descent to the underworld to wake the souls of the dead and take them to heaven is what is understood as "the descent into hell." The image of this is wonderfully captured in an ancient homily that the church now uses as one of its readings for the hour of vigils on Holy Saturday.

But that's an image, something that captures, as might an icon, a deeper reality. It's not a videotape of an actual happening. How is it to be interpreted? How did Jesus descend into hell?

Let me try to explain this by combining three images:

The first is a story, a tragic one: Some years ago some family friends of mine lost a daughter to suicide. She was in her early twenties and away from home when she made her first attempt to kill herself. The family rushed to her, flew her home, surrounded her with loving solicitude, took her to doctors of every kind, and generally tried every possible way to love and coax her out of her deadly depression. In the end, they failed. She killed herself, despite their efforts. All the loving effort and professional resources they could muster could not break through and bring her out of the private hell into which she had descended. Strong as human love can be, sometimes it stands helpless, exhausted, before a door it can't open.

My second image is taken from John's Gospel: After Jesus rises from the dead, he appears to the disciples who, as John describes, are huddled together in a room, in fear, with the doors locked. Jesus comes right through the locked doors, stands inside the middle of their fear, and breathes out peace. A week later, he does it again (John 20:19, 26).

A third image: When I was a young boy, my mother gave me a holy card, an adaptation of a famous painting by Holman Hunt, "The Light of the World." In the version my mother gave me, we see, behind a locked door, a man huddled and paralyzed by a fear and darkness of some kind. Outside the door stands Jesus, with a lantern, knocking, ready to relieve the man of his burden. But there's a hitch: The door has a knob only on the inside. Jesus cannot enter, unless the man first unlocks the door. There's the implication that God cannot help unless we first let God in. Fair enough? Not exactly.

What the cross of Christ reveals is that when we are so paralyzed by fear and overcome by darkness that we can no longer help ourselves, when we have reached the stage where we can no longer open the door to let light and life in, God can still come through our locked doors, stand inside our fear and paralysis, and breathe out peace. The love that is revealed in Jesus's suffering and death, a love that is so other-centered that it can fully forgive and embrace its executioners, can pass through locked doors, melt frozen hearts, penetrate the walls of fear, and descend into our private hells and, precisely there, breathe out peace.

In the case of the young woman who committed suicide, she had reached a point where she was frozen inside of a private hell, behind doors that her family's love and professional doctors could no longer open. They stood outside of her locked doors, like Jesus in Holman Hunt's painting, knocking, begging for a response that she could no longer give. I have no doubt though that when she awoke on the other side she found Christ standing inside her fear and darkness, breathing out peace.

The doctrine of the "descent into hell" is singularly the most consoling of all doctrines, in any religion. As that ancient homily on Holy Saturday so wonderfully puts it, the love that Christ reveals in the cross is so strong that it can descend into any hell we can create, thaw out our frozen souls, and lead us into the light and peace of paradise, despite our fears and weaknesses. The cross of Christ does not stand helpless before a locked door.

CHAPTER FOUR

The Cross as Salvation—"Being Washed in the Blood of the Lamb"

Some Metaphors and Icons

I t is easier to grasp what the cross teaches us about God and God's unconditional love than it is to understand how the cross brings us salvation. How, through what one man suffered centuries ago, are we saved today, two thousand years later? This seems impossible to explain and yet that belief is central to the Christian faith. We are all, as the primary symbol in our theology of salvation teaches, washed clean in the blood of the lamb. But how does that work? How did Jesus's death open the gates of heaven for us and pay the debt for our sins? How is Jesus the "lamb of God" who takes away our sins and the sins of the world?

Scripture answers this by offering us a great variety of metaphors. Here are a number of them:

"He paid the price for our sins." "We are saved by his blood." "He paid the debt of sin." "We are washed clean in the blood of the lamb." "The lamb of God takes away our sins." "He restored us to life, after our death in Adam's sin." "He conquered death, once and for all." "By his stripes we were healed." "He offered an eternal sacrifice." "He is our victim." "He opened the gates of heaven." "He stripped the principalities and Satan of their power."

It is important to remember that these are to be taken as metaphors, as icons to contemplate, and not as literal descriptions of something. Jesus is clearly not a sheep and God did not want and script Jesus's death as payment, in pain, for Adam's sin and ours. In the Gospels, Jesus never speaks of his death as a ransom payment for sins, but rather always as a gift of love.

So how can we understand this? How are we, today, saved through the death of Jesus some two thousand years ago? How does Jesus's death atone for our sins?

Partly this is a mystery, a truth that lies beyond us. But that partial ineffability is a positive thing. Love, too, is always partially a mystery. Any truth that we can fully grasp and understand is, in the end, not very deep. The deepest truths are always somewhat beyond us. But, because they are always partially ineffable, this does not mean that we cannot know them, and know them profoundly; it only means that we cannot intellectually grasp them and articulate satisfactorily their phenomenology. Simply put, there isn't a theologian in the world who can give us an adequate explanation of how the death of Jesus, two thousand years ago, washes away and atones for our sins. Yet, every Christian, to the extent that we have faith, has an intuitive, gut-sense of what that means. And to the extent that we have a genuine Christian faith we, in fact, risk our lives and our faith upon that truth. This is captured in the statement of the young woman interviewed by *Time* magazine, whom we quoted earlier, when she says that as she witnessed her mother being murdered and saw her blood on the wall and the mattress, she knew, in her gut, that somehow her mother's blood and Jesus's blood were one and the same, and that somehow Jesus's death gave dignity to her mother's death. In effect, she said: *I don't understand it, but I get it!* She then adds that realizing the deep connection between her mother's death and Jesus's death has prompted her to study theology and become a minister in her church. In essence, she knows the mystery well enough, without understanding it, to live her whole life upon its truth.

It is the same with us. This is a profound mystery, partially beyond our grasp, but we intuit its truth so strongly that it becomes the deepest truth in our lives. Hence the passageway to understanding how Jesus is the Lamb of God who takes away our sins is accessed more through metaphor, icon, and contemplation than it is through intellectual concepts. It is something we grasp with our hearts more than with our heads.

After searching through books for more than forty years looking for a satisfactory explanation, I am content at this stage of my life to contemplate this truth as I would a beautiful icon. It is something I need to look at again and again, in contemplation, asking it to reveal to me the deep truth that it symbolically embodies. I leave you with two such "icons" upon which to reflect. The first is from the renowned Scripture scholar C.H. Dodd and the second is from the Trappist monk Thomas Keating.

Describing Jesus's death, C.H. Dodd makes this comment:

> There was more here than could be accounted for upon the historical or human level. God was in it. The creative purpose of God is everlastingly at work in this world of his. It meets resistance from the recalcitrant wills of men. If at any point human history should become entirely nonresistant to God, perfectly transparent to his design—then from that point the creative purpose would work with unprecedented power. That is just what the perfect obedience of Jesus effected. Within human nature and human history he established a point of complete nonresistance to the will of God, and

complete transparency to his design. As we revert to that moment, it becomes contemporary and we are laid open to the creative energy perpetually working to make man after the image of God. The obedience of Christ is the release of creative power for the perfecting of human life. A decision taken by a great man or woman can alter every aspect of life, for the present and for all that comes after.[4]

Thomas Keating offers this comment in response to a question: Have we ever really understood how we are saved by Jesus's death more than two centuries ago?

Scripture provides examples of persons who actually had an insight into this—for instance, Mary of Bethany, anointing Jesus at Simon the leper's house. By breaking the alabaster jar of very expensive perfume over the whole body of Jesus and filling the house with that gorgeous scent, she seems to have intuited what Jesus was about to do on the cross. The authorities were set on killing him. What her lavish gesture symbolized was the deepest meaning of Jesus's passion and death. The body of Christ is the jar containing the most precious perfume of all time, namely, the Holy Spirit. It was about to be broken open so that the Holy Spirit could be poured out over the whole of humanity—past, present, and to come—with boundless generosity. Until that body had been broken on the cross, the full extent of the gift of God in Christ and its transforming possibilities for the human race could not be known or remotely foreseen.[5]

Jesus as Taking Away the Sins of the World

How Jesus's death takes away our sins is, as we just saw, always partially a mystery. However there are some aspects of this that can be more rationally articulated and these offer us, I believe, a powerful challenge to participate in the saving activity of Jesus's death.

In trying to answer how Jesus is the Lamb of God who takes away our sins, we should be careful not to fall into a common misunderstanding. Because of certain biblical and doctrinal ways of expressing this, the impression can be given that Jesus's suffering and death took away the sins of the world by somehow paying off a debt to God, namely, that God took Jesus's suffering as compensation for our sin—implying that God had lived in anger since Adam's sin, waiting for someone to adequately pay the debt before that sin could be forgiven. The images and metaphors used to express Jesus's expiation for sin can, if taken literally, give that impression, but that is not what they mean. What do they mean?

There is a rich background to this concept: Many pre-Christian cultures had rituals involving a scapegoat. It was not enacted the same way in every place, but in essence it went something like this: At regular intervals, a community would try to purge itself of the evils that were besetting it (divisions, rivalries, jealousies, violence, warfare, theft, anger, murder, and the like) by a ritual designed to take these things out of the community. The ritual had this format: They would take a goat and would, through some symbols (which often included draping the goat in purple and putting a crown of thorns on its head), figuratively load on its back all that they felt was wrong inside their community. The goat was then driven out into the desert to die. The idea was that the goat was taking the sin of the community away with it. Curiously, this generally had a certain effectiveness. For a time afterward, there would more unity within the group.

Of course no real transformation took place. Nothing really changed. Jealousies and anger remained as before, even if for a time people were able to live together more harmoniously. A goat, driven into the desert to die, does not take sin out of a community. How then does Jesus, as the Lamb slain, take sin out of a community?

Jesus, as the Lamb of God, does not take away the sin of the world by somehow carrying it off so that it is no longer present inside of the community. Nor does he take it away by paying off a debt to God for Adam's sin and ours. He takes it away by transforming it, by taking it inside of him and not giving it back. An image can be helpful in explaining this: What Jesus did in his death, in the way he died in love, is analogous to what a water filter does. It takes in water that contains impurities, dirt, toxins, and occasional poisons. The filter does not simply let the water flow through it, as does an electrical cord; rather the water filter *holds the dirt and toxins inside of itself and gives back only the pure water.* In simple language, Jesus took away the sin of the world by taking in hatred and giving back love; by taking in anger and giving out graciousness; by taking in envy and giving back blessing; by taking in bitterness and giving out warmth; by taking in pettiness and giving back compassion; by taking in chaos and giving back peace; and by taking in sin and giving back forgiveness.

What Jesus illustrates in his death is how a sin-purifier works inside of life. Sin is taken away not by some scapegoat carrying it off and away from the community. Rather, Jesus's death took away sin by absorbing it, by eating the tension and not conducting it—like a water purifier when it cleans water. We see examples of this throughout his entire life, although it is most manifest in the love and forgiveness he shows at the time of his death. Hence, immediately after his death, his followers recognized this and applied the concept of the scape-goat, the lamb who takes away the tension of the community, to him. Except that they recognized that, in Jesus's case, it actually worked: the tension and sin actually were taken away.

What is most important here is that this is not something we are asked to simply admire. We are asked to imitate it, to do in our lives what Jesus did and, in this way, keep incarnate the Lamb of God who takes away the sins of the world. We are asked to go into our families, communities, churches, and civil society, where always there is tension, and become the shock absorbers and water filters that absorb the sin and don't give it back. Our task, too, is to help take away the sins of the world. We do this whenever we take in hatred, anger, envy, pettiness, and bitterness and hold them, transmute them, and eventually give them back as love, graciousness, blessing, compassion, warmth, and forgiveness.

Whenever we do this, the Lamb of God is still taking away the sins of the world, thousands of years later.

Of course, this is not an easy thing to do. What comes naturally is to give back in kind: hatred for hatred, anger for anger, coldness for coldness, revenge for hurt. Someone hits us so we hit back. But then sin stays inside the community and no amount of scapegoating, ritualized in liturgy or otherwise, is of any real value in changing things because we are not transforming anything but are simply acting as conduits, passing on the identical energy that is pressed upon us. Jesus did otherwise. He did not simply pass on what was done to him. Rather he took it in, held it, carried it, transformed it, and eventually gave it back as something else. This is what constitutes the sacrificial part of his love; namely, the *excruciating* pain (*ex cruce*, from "the cross") that he had to undergo in order to take in hatred and give back love. But that is the only way that sin can ever leave a community; someone has to take it in, hold it, carry it, and, through a certain excruciating sacrifice of self, transform it into something else. For this reason Christianity, among all the religions and philosophies of the world, is the only one that worships the scapegoat.

A further comment is still needed on this question. There's a centuries-old question that asks why Jesus had to die in so horrible a manner. Why all this blood? What kind of cosmic and divine game is being played out here? Is Christ's blood, the blood of the lamb, somehow paying someone off for the sin of Adam and Eve and for our own sins? Why does blood need to be spilled?

This is a complex question and every answer that can be given is only a very partial one. We are dealing with the greatest of all mysteries here. However one of the reasons why Jesus dies in this way—one of the reasons for all the blood—is clear, and its implications are profound. It has precisely to do with blood.

From the beginning of time right up until the crucifixion of Jesus, all cultures sacrificed blood to their gods. Why blood? Because blood is so strongly identified with the life-principle. Blood carries life, is life, and its loss is death. Thus it shouldn't be surprising to us that everywhere in ancient cultures the idea was present that what we owe to God is blood, that God needs blood. In their view of things, blood was the only language that God really understood. So they felt that they should be offering blood to God. And they did. For a long time, this included human blood. Humans were killed on altars everywhere. Eventually, however, many cultures eliminated human sacrifice and used animals instead. By the time of Jesus, the Temple had become a giant butchery with priests killing animals nearly nonstop. Some scholars suggest that when Jesus upset the money changers' tables in the Temple, about 90 percent of commerce in Jerusalem was in one way or the other connected with animal sacrifice. No wonder Jesus's action was perceived as a threat!

So why all that blood at Jesus's death? Because, as Franciscan author Richard Rohr suggests, for all these centuries we have been spilling blood to try to get to God and, in the crucifixion, things get reversed:

God spills his own blood to try to get to us. It's this reversal that rips open the old veil of fear, the false belief that God wants blood. God does not want us to spill blood to get to God. We are not meant to live in fear of God, and all the blood in the crucifixion of Jesus is meant to tell us that.

Jesus's Last Words—"It Is Finished"

There is another reason why Jesus's death still echoes, more than two thousand years later. Just before he dies on the cross, Jesus utters these words: "It is finished!"

What's "finished"?

These words can be spoken in different ways: They can be words of defeat and despair: "It's over, hopeless, I give in!" Conversely they can be words of accomplishment and triumph: "I've done it, succeeded, I've held out!"

Obviously, for Jesus, these are not words of defeat. He has triumphed, succeeded, run the toughest race of all to its finish. When he speaks these words, he's like the winner in the Olympic marathon throwing up his arms in triumph at the finish line; except in this case both his exuberance of spirit and his arms are nailed down so that his utterance of triumph is not like the fist-pump of an Olympic winner, but like the cry of an newborn baby that's finally succeeded in pushing itself through the birth canal. It is a startling triumph, but one that, for a time, has the victor lying in blood, tears, and helplessness.

And his triumph here left him precisely in blood, tears, and help-lessness. He's won, but it's cost him his life, tested his faith to the limit, lost him his popularity, scattered his friends, shrouded his life in misunderstanding, left him looking compromised, and isolated him in an unspeakable loneliness.

It's not easy then to pump your fist in triumph, even when you've won, especially since your victory isn't evident to anyone who isn't journeying inside of this with you. To everyone else, this looks like defeat, the worst kind of defeat.

So what's "finished"?

At one level, what's finished is Jesus's own struggle with doubt, fear, and loneliness. What was that struggle? The painful, lonely, crushing discrepancy he habitually felt between the warmth and ideals inside his heart and the coldness and despair he met in the world.

Everything inside of him believed that, in the end, always, it is better to give yourself over to love than to hatred, to affirmation than to jealousy, to gentleness of heart than to bitterness, to honesty than to lying, to fidelity than to compromise, to forgiveness than to revenge. Everything about him too was a testimony that the reality of God, immaterial and fanciful though it can seem, is in the end more real than the undeniable reality of our physical bodies and our physical world. And finally, everything about him pointed uncompromisingly toward the "road less taken" and revealed that real love means carrying your solitude and chastity at a high level.

But for him, as for us, it wasn't easy to live that out. As Scripture says, sometimes it gets dark in the middle of the day, sometimes we find ourselves very much alone in what we believe in, and sometimes God seems far away and dead. Faith and love aren't easy because they feel empty and fanciful whenever they're betrayed. Only when they're persevered in will they work and prove that they're real.

Jesus, though, did persevere in them, and when he utters the words, "It is finished," it's a statement of triumph, not just of his own faith, but of love, truth, and God. He's taken God at his word, risked everything on faith and, despite the pain it's brought, is dying with no regrets. The struggle for faith, for him, is finished. He's succeeded; he's crossed the finish line.

But there's second level of meaning to his words. "It is finished" also means that the reign of sin and death is finished. It is the end of an order of things wherein we live our lives believing that everyday joys eventually give way to darkness and the underworld, paranoia and sin unmask trust and goodness as naïve, the reality of the physical world and this life is all there is, compromise and infidelity trump everything else, and death is more real than hope. This order is also finished; it is exposed as unreal, as a lie, by love, fidelity, gentleness, trust, childlikeness, vulnerability, and the paradoxical power of a God who, in the deeper recesses of things, works more by underwhelming than by overpowering.

"It is finished!" Jesus uttered those words when he realized that, despite all the pain and sin in the world, the center does hold, love can be trusted, God is real, and, because of that, in the end, "every manner of being shall be well" as Julian of Norwich puts it. The forces of sin and death are finished because we can, in full maturity and utter realism, believe in the sun even when it isn't shining, in love even when we don't feel it, and in God, even when God is silent. Faith and God deliver on their promise.

Mohandas Gandhi in a remarkable passage once wrote: "When I despair, I remember that all through history, the way of truth and love has always won. There have been murderers and tyrants, and for a time they can seem invincible. But in the end they always fall. Think of it, always."[6]

Many things were finished on the cross, including rule of tyranny and murder.

Jesus's Death as Releasing Blood and Water

And what else continues to flow from Jesus's death after all these centuries?

The Gospel of John tells us that at the moment of Jesus's death "blood and water" flowed from his dead body. This is a stunning image carrying several levels of meaning. First of all, the image is clearly one of birth: blood and water accompany the newborn out of the womb. Jesus's death is understood to be giving birth to something in the world. What is being born? The answer is in the symbols.

What is blood? Blood is the life-principle inside us. We are alive when blood flows through us. What is water? Water does two things for us, it quenches thirst and it washes us clean. When we combine these concepts, we begin to get a sense of what the Gospel is trying to teach us here. It is telling us what Jesus's disciples experienced inside themselves in the face of his death. They felt an outpouring of blood and water; that is, a deeper and richer flow of life within themselves and a sense of being both nurtured and cleansed in a new way. They felt something flow out from Jesus's death that made them freer, less guilty, and more open to life than ever before. They felt washed, cleansed, and nourished.

This sounds abstract and quasi-magical, but it is anything but that. We, too, have the same experience when someone we know and love dies in such a way so as to give his or her death to us. An example can help explicate this: If someone were to ask me this question: What were the happiest occasions that you have been present to within the last ten years? My answer would at first glance seem curious: a number of funerals. The happiest occasions that I have been present to within the last decade were a number of specific funerals, funerals of persons, women and men, who, in the way they died, figuratively set off a flow of blood and water from their caskets.

To cite one such example: A couple of years ago, I went to visit a man who was already in palliative care, dying of cancer. He was a young man, still in his fifties, but he was dying well because he was dying in the same way as he had lived his life, without bitterness and without enemies. He spoke to me of the intense loneliness of dying and then he shared this: "I've had a good life and I've no regrets. I don't think I have an enemy, at least I don't know of one. And, I want to do this right. I want to die with a dignity that makes my wife and kids proud of me. I want to do this right for them and for everyone else."

He died some days later and his family and everyone else who knew him were deeply saddened. But, inside that sadness, there was also something else, an outflow of blood and water. After his funeral, as we walked out of church to a small reception, there was not one person who knew this man well, including his grieving wife and children, who, at a level deeper than the sadness of the moment, did not feel freer, less guilty, and more open to life than ever before. He wanted to do his death right, and he did, and that reinforced everything good he had done in his life so that what he wanted to give to us came to us, the goodness of his life and the love he showed in his death. Blood and water flowed from his casket, to all of us and not least to his family.

Less happily, this is also sometimes true in its opposite: Not every death is a gift to those who knew that person. All of us have also been to funerals where, because of the manner in which the person lived or died, we did not feel blood and water flowing from the casket but rather felt as if the very oxygen was being drawn out of the room. Instead of feeling freer, less guilty, and more open to life, we felt guilty about the very act of breathing and guilty about enjoying anything in life.

How we live and how we die leaves behind a spirit, a blessing or a curse, after we are gone. Our caskets will either emit a flow of life-giving and guilt-freeing blood and water, or they will suck some of the oxygen from the room and the hearts of those who knew us.

In the way Jesus died for us, blood and water, oxygen and life, have been poured out, forever, on this earth.

Standing with Mary under the Cross

One of the most popular images in all of Scripture, an icon that's been endlessly painted, sung, put into litanies, written up into poetry, and used to triggered every kind of piety, is the image of Mary, the mother of Jesus, standing silently under the cross as her son dies.

As Jesus was dying, the Gospels tell us that Mary, his mother, stood under the cross. What's in that image? What's in this picture that invites us to more than simple admiration, piety, or sympathy?

This is a mystical image and it is anything but pious. In the Gospels, after Jesus, Mary is the most important person to watch. She's the model of discipleship, the only one who gets it right. And she gets it very right under the cross. What's she doing while standing there?

On the surface, it seems she isn't doing anything at all: She doesn't speak, she doesn't try to stop the crucifixion, and she doesn't even protest its unfairness or plead Jesus's innocence. She is mute, seemingly passive, overtly doing nothing. But at a deeper level, she is doing all that can be done when one is standing under the weight of the cross: She's holding the tension, standing in strength, refusing to give back in kind, and resisting in a deeper way.

What's meant by this?

Sometimes well-intentioned artists have painted Mary as lying prostrate under the cross: the wounded mother, helplessly distraught, paralyzed in grief, an object for sympathy. But that doesn't honor what happened there nor teach its lesson. Prostration, in this situation, is weakness, collapse, hysteria, resignation. In the Gospels, "standing" is the opposite—a position of strength. Mary "stood" under the cross.

Still, why the silence and why her seeming unwillingness to act or protest?

In essence, what Mary was doing under the cross was this: She couldn't stop the crucifixion (there are times when darkness has its hour) but she could stop some of the hatred, bitterness, jealousy, heartlessness, and anger that caused it and surrounded it. And she helped stop bitterness by refusing to give it back in kind, by transforming rather than transmitting it, by swallowing hard and (literally) eating bitterness rather than giving it back, as everyone else was doing.

Had Mary, in moral outrage, begun to scream hysterically, shout angrily at those crucifying Jesus, or physically tried to attack someone as he was driving the nails into Jesus's hands, she would have been caught up in the same kind of energy as everyone else, replicating the very anger and bitterness that caused the crucifixion to begin with. What Mary was doing under the cross, her silence and seeming unwillingness to protest notwithstanding, was radiating all that is antithetical to the crucifixion: gentleness, understanding, forgiveness, peace, light.

And that's not easy to do. Everything inside us demands justice, screams for it, and refuses to remain silent in the presence of injustice. That's a healthy instinct and sometimes acting on it is good. We need, at times, to protest, to shout, to literally throw ourselves into the face of injustice and do everything in our power to stop the crucifixion.

But there are times too when things have gone so far that shouts and protests are no longer helpful, darkness is going to have its hour and all we can do is to stand under the cross and help eat its bitterness by refusing to participate in its energy. In those situations, like Mary, we have to say: "I can't stop this crucifixion, but I can stop some of the hatred, bitterness, jealousy, brutality, heartlessness, and darkness that surround it. I can't stop this injustice, but I will not conduct its hatred."

And that's not the same thing as despair. Our muted helplessness is not a passive resignation but the opposite. It's a movement toward the only rays of light, love, and faith that still exist in that darkness and hatred. And, at that moment, it's the only thing that faith and love can do.

As the book of Lamentations says, there are times when the best we can do is "put one's mouth to the dust" and wait! (Lamentations 3:29). Sometimes too, as the poet Rainer Maria Rilke says, the only helpful thing is to absorb the heaviness:

Do not be afraid to suffer, give
the heaviness back to the weight of the earth;
mountains are heavy, seas are heavy.[7]

That's not passivity, resignation, or weakness: It's genuine, rare strength. It's "standing under the cross" so as to help take away some of its hatred, chaos, bitterness, and violence.

So this is the image: Sometimes darkness has its hour and there is nothing we can do to stop it. Sometimes the blind, wounded forces of jealousy, bitterness, violence, and sin cannot, for that moment, be stopped. But, like Mary under the cross, we are asked to "stand" under them, not in passivity and weakness, but in strength, knowing that we can't stop the crucifixion but we can help stop some of the hatred, anger, and bitterness that surround it.

And, in this way, we help take away the sins of the world and continue to bring Jesus's saving death to the world.

Carrying Our Cross in Imitation of Jesus

Among Jesus's many teachings we find this rather harsh-sounding, invitation: "If any want to become my followers, let them deny themselves and take up their cross daily and follow me. For those who want to save their life will lose it, and those who lose their life for my sake will save it" (Luke 9:23–24).

I suspect that each of us has a gut-sense of what this means and what it will cost us; but, I suspect too that many of us misunderstand what Jesus is asking here and struggle unhealthily with this invitation. What, concretely, does Jesus mean by this?

To answer that, I would like to lean on some insights offered by James Martin in his book *Jesus: A Pilgrimage*. He suggests that taking up our cross daily and giving up life in order to find deeper life means six interpenetrating things:

First, it means accepting that suffering is a part of our lives. Accepting our cross and giving up our lives means that, at some point, we have to make peace with the unalterable fact that frustration, disappointment, pain, misfortune, illness, unfairness, sadness, and death are a part of our lives and they must ultimately be accepted without bitterness. As long as we nurse the notion that pain in our lives is something we need not accept, we will habitually find ourselves bitter—bitter for not having accepted the cross.

Second, taking up our cross and giving up our lives means that we may not, in our suffering, pass on any bitterness to those around us. We have a strong inclination, almost as part of our natural instincts, to make others suffer when we are suffering: "If I'm unhappy, I will make sure that others around me are unhappy too!" This does not mean, as Martin points out, that we cannot share our pain with others. But there's a healthy way of doing this, where our sharing leaves others free, as opposed to an unhealthy kind of sharing that subtly tries to make others unhappy because we are unhappy. There's a difference between healthily groaning under the weight of our pain and unhealthily whining in self-pity and bitterness under that weight.

The cross gives us permission to do the former, but not the latter. Jesus groaned under the weight of his cross, but no self-pity, whining, or bitterness issued forth from his lips or his beaten body.

Third, walking in the footsteps of Jesus as he carries his cross means that we must accept some other deaths before our physical death, that we are invited to let some parts of ourselves die. When Jesus invites us to die in order to find life, he is not, first of all, talking about physical death. If we live in adulthood, there are a myriad of other deaths that we must undergo before we die physically. Maturity and Christian discipleship are about perennially naming our deaths, claiming our births, mourning our losses, letting go of what's died, and receiving new spirit for the new life that we are now living. These are the stages of the paschal mystery, and the stages of growing up. There are daily deaths.

Fourth, it means that we must wait for the resurrection, that here in this life all symphonies must remain unfinished. So much of life and discipleship is about waiting—waiting in frustration, inside injustice, inside pain, in longing, battling bitterness—as we wait for something or someone to come and change our situation. We spend about 98 percent of our lives waiting for fulfillment, in small and big ways. Jesus's invitation to us to follow him implies waiting and accepting the truth that we live inside an unfinished symphony.

Fifth, carrying our cross daily means accepting that God's gift to us is often not what we expect. God always answers our prayers but, oftentimes, by giving us what we really need rather than what we think we need. Resurrection, says James Martin, does not come when we expect it and rarely fits our notion of how a resurrection should happen. To carry your cross is to be open to surprise.

Finally, taking up your cross and being willing to give up your life means living in a faith that believes that nothing is impossible for God. As James Martin puts it, this means accepting that God is greater than the human imagination. Indeed, whenever we succumb to the notion that God cannot offer us a way out of our pain into some kind of newness, it's precisely because we have reduced God down to the size of our own limited imagination. It's possible to accept our cross, to live in trust, and to not grow bitter inside pain only if we believe in possibilities beyond what we can imagine; namely, if we believe in the resurrection.

Helping Simon of Cyrene to Carry the Cross

It seems as though through purely earthly accidents we are made responsible for what is heavenly and divine.

Karl Rahner wrote words to this effect to describe what happened to St. Joseph when he was asked by an angel to be the husband to Mary and support her in the birth and raising of Jesus. Something of God was entrusted into his care, but not because he wanted it, planned it, or because he himself was central to the event. He was asked to do something simply because of circumstance, because he was engaged to someone inside a great drama. Moreover, what he was asked to do radically reshaped his life in a way not according to his own choosing.

Rahner's words are just as accurate when applied to Simon of Cyrene, the man conscripted to help Jesus carry his cross. The passion accounts tell us that, when Jesus was too weak and weary to carry the cross, a passerby, Simon of Cyrene, was forced to help him carry it (see Mark 15:21).

We aren't given any details as to how this happened other than that Simon was someone who was incidentally there, a "passerby," a victim of circumstance. This was not something for which he had planned or volunteered. He was merely at the wrong place at the wrong time. No doubt too, being conscripted to help carry the cross was an irritation and something humbling and shameful for him (guilt by association with a condemned criminal). Helping a scorned person carry his or her humiliation in front of a jeering crowd doesn't exactly bring the same reaction as helping a world-champion golfer carry his golf clubs in front of adoring fans.

Whatever Simon's feelings, there can be no doubt that helping Jesus carry his cross was something that was unwanted, unpleasant, and was experienced at the time as an unfairness or bad luck.

Yet, ironically, this would be the most significant thing he would do in his whole life, earning him a place in history and folklore that can only be envied by the most famous of athletes, entertainers, politicians, writers, and religious figures. Simon of Cyrene will forever be famous. Thousands of years from now his name will still be remembered, and for the right reason: He helped carry the cross of Jesus.

There's a wonderful mystical image here; namely, the picture of a man or woman being victimized by circumstance so that he or she, simply by being at a given place at a given time, is conscripted to do a task that is unwanted, unplanned for, humbling, and disruptive of his or her own agenda and dreams. And yet this unwanted thing becomes, in the end, the most important thing he or she will ever do.

How does that happen to you? How do you become a Simon of Cyrene, helping Jesus carry his cross?

The cross of Jesus appears in many forms:

• Whenever you are the one who has to take care of an aging parent because circumstance arranges that you are the one who happens to be living close by.

• Whenever you are the parent of a handicapped child and are asked to do things ordinary parents aren't asked to do.

• Whenever you are the one to whom the emotionally needy person at work chooses to reach out.

• Whenever you are the one whose gentle nature makes it difficult to say no and people take advantage of you.

• Whenever you are the one who is the first at the scene of an accident.

• Whenever you are the one whom the drunk accosts on the sidewalk.

• Whenever you are the one who forever finds herself caught up in duties not of her own choosing that always have you around when the less glamorous work needs to be done.

• Whenever you are the one whose plans and dreams can be sacrificed because everyone else's are deemed more important.

• Whenever you're the one whose life is disrupted by unwanted circumstance, you are Simon of Cyrene, helping Jesus carry the cross.

Simon of Cyrene was not central to the drama or meaning of Jesus's passion and death. He was an unimportant figure who happened to be standing at the edges of things when the drama accidentally enfolded him and forced him to play an unglamorous, self-effacing, but needed role. His own agenda and plans had to be sacrificed and his response was, no doubt, less than fully enthusiastic. Yet this unplanned for, conscripted, humble service became the most important thing he ever did, his signature piece, and gave him a place in history beyond the thousands and millions whose place in the drama of life was once deemed important.

Henri Nouwen once said, "I used to get upset about all the interruptions to my work until one day I realized that the interruptions *were* my real work." Pure earthly accidents often do make us responsible for what is divine, and they conscript us to our real work—helping Simon of Cyrene carry the cross of Jesus.

The Cross's Presence to Us in our Humiliations

One of the characteristics of divine revelation is that it often breaks through where you least expect. Grace invariably catches you unaware—a surprise. Frequently, too, that surprise is not a pleasant one, for God shines brightly in our humiliations, unafraid to be embarrassed in this world.

Let me risk an example: At age fifteen, Thérèse of Lisieux made the decision to enter a Carmelite monastery. She thought she had prepared herself fairly well for what she would meet there, and indeed she had. She was under no illusion about what lay ahead for her, both in terms of the austerity of the life she was taking on as well as in terms of how some of the nuns would react toward her. She knew it would be hard: early rising, long hours in chapel, poor food, inadequate heating, a small cell with a straw mattress, days spent mainly in silence, hard menial work, rules forbidding her at times to talk to her own blood sisters, and little or nothing in the way of earthly compensation. She was even prepared for the fact that many of the nuns would react badly toward her: questioning her motivation, seeing her as a spoiled child, misunderstanding her vocation, treating her with coldness or, alternately, doting on her as the community baby. She had thought all of this through beforehand and felt ready for whatever met her in that monastery. Thus when she entered its gates, she was well-prepared, ready for everything—except what actually happened.

Shortly after she walked through the gates of that convent, her father—whom she adored, and who had loved her purely and deeply and had throughout her whole life radiated the love and compassion of God—went insane. Moreover, his insanity (a form of mental illness not understood at the time) led him to do strange, humiliating things. He became as helpless as a child, constantly got lost, had inexplicable mood swings, grew silent, reacted angrily at times without cause, could not be trusted to be alone, did embarrassing things, and was once even caught by the police carrying a revolver. Thérèse had idealized this man and had been very proud of him. For her, until now, he had embodied God. He had been, for her, as loving, as stable, as predictable in goodness, and as utterly trustworthy as God. Initially, therefore, her father's insanity shattered her world entirely (not just in terms of her family life but also, and especially, in her understanding of God). How could someone so trustworthy, good, stable, and loving suddenly become so different? Beyond that too, some of her relatives blamed her for her father's illness, saying that her leaving him for the convent had broken his heart. It took a long time, a lot of pondering, and a much deeper understanding of God, before Thérèse was able to make her peace with all of this.

Eventually, however, she learned something from this experience that profoundly reshaped her spirituality. What she learned was this: To know God, one must begin to grasp the humiliation of God in this world. What is implied in this? Where do we see the humiliation of God in this world?

Whenever we see someone who is unable to protect herself or himself against pain, especially the type of pain that humbles and humiliates, we are witnessing the humiliation of God in the world and if we have the eyes of faith we are standing at that place where the deeper secrets of heaven are being revealed.

We see this clearly when we look at little children. They are so helpless and needy that they cannot hide what needs to be hidden. Spittle, urine, mucus, feces, and tears are always in evidence around them. We see this too whenever we see anyone who, for whatever reason, is perceived by others as naïve, unattractive, stupid, irrational—or in some other way is seen as an embarrassment to himself or herself. And we see it especially in those people who because of age or illness are being humiliated in their bodies. In an adult body ravaged by age, handicap, or terminal disease—unlike the case of babies where a stunning physical beauty and wholeness more than compensate for the embarrassment and where the smell of feces can be sweet—there is real humiliation. Here the smell of feces is not sweet.

I recently visited a friend dying of cancer. Her fifty-year-old body, once remarkably beautiful, was grossly disfigured, wasted, smelled of death, and, like the face of the Suffering Servant in Isaiah, was as much an object of revulsion as of attraction. A proud spirit, she lay humble, embarrassed, humiliated in her body. But God lay with her in that humiliation, shining forth, revealing secrets, tearing the temple veil from top to bottom and revealing what was revealed on the cross: namely, that faith and understanding begin at that exact dark point where the world thinks it must end.

The Embrace of Good Friday

There are different kinds of loneliness, just as there are different visions of intimacy. We ache in many places, just as we dream various dreams of consummation.

I remember as a young priest, just ordained and barely beyond the loneliness of adolescence, saying Mass and feeling very deeply these words from the Eucharistic Prayer: "Grant that we, who are nourished by his body and blood, may be filled with his Holy Spirit, and become one body, one spirit in Christ" (Eucharistic Prayer III). I would say those words back then and they would excite my romantic imagination and incite feelings and fantasies that had to do with the fulfillment of my own personal loneliness. To become one body in Christ connoted, for me, that embrace that would put an end to my endless aching, restlessness, and sexual inconsummation. The need for unity in Christ, as I felt it then, had to do with my own personal distance from others.

That was the loneliness I felt then and that was what, by and large, I most wanted from the Eucharist (which I have always believed to be an embrace). I'm no longer a young priest and, although I cannot confidently state that I am beyond the loneliness of adolescence (who is?), I feel those words of the Eucharist quite differently now. When I now pray that Christ should make us one body, it is not so much my personal loneliness that I want overcome as it is something much wider, something beyond just me and my own aches and inconsummations. What I now feel more strongly is how painfully separate, and separated, we all are from each other and how seemingly hopeless are the divisions among us.

I pray the Eucharistic Prayer now and what I feel, first of all, is not my own romantic and sexual separateness but how torn is our world and everything in it, myself included. How separate we are! How divided we are! History, circumstance, background, temperament, ideology, gender, race, geography, and religion, among other things, make it difficult and seemingly hopeless, for us ever to be one. There is a loneliness and inconsummation in the whole world. The world aches, as did my adolescent self.

Moreover, the older I get, the more I despair of any simple solution to this. There will not be world community, world peace, and one body simply because we sincerely desire it. The divisions among us—like the issues that separate a man and a woman who can no longer fight through the things that divide them and are asking for a divorce—are too overpowering. We too, as a world, no longer can find a way to embrace one another that will heal all the hurt and stop the divisions. We need an embrace from beyond, a vision from beyond, an intimacy we cannot give to ourselves.

Jesus, dying on the cross, is that embrace, that vision, that intimacy. We look at a cross and we see the secret. That is what a real reconciling embrace looks like. We don't understand it; we see it. And what do we see there?

A man, a God, hangs naked, exposed, vulnerable, defenseless, silent, with his arms stretched wide, open for an embrace, and with his hands also stretched open with nails driven through them. Yet strangely, in all that, we don't see bitterness, defeat, and anger. Paradoxically, we see their opposite. This is what real trust, love, and metanoia (*un-para-noia*) look like.

And I say "look like" because we don't understand this—we see it. We don't understand intellectually how giving oneself over in betrayal teaches trust, nor how vulnerability and powerlessness are the real powers that bring about intimacy. But we *see* this when we look at the cross of Jesus. It is no wonder that so many people— millions, literally—wear a cross as a symbol of love, trust, and hope. Unconsciously, they know, however dimly, what theology can never quite make clear to us: namely, that what divides us from each other can only be bridged by the cross of Christ, and that our hope for intimacy and community is not in ourselves but in an embrace that is beyond us. In a cross this is not understood, it's seen—mystically, not rationally.

So, as a priest, I stand daily before an altar and pray the words: "Grant that we, who are nourished by his body and blood, may be filled with his Holy Spirit, and become one body, one spirit in Christ." What I pray for is precisely that what we see in the cross of Christ actually might be given to us: namely, an embrace from beyond ourselves.

In the cross lies the answer to our loneliness. It was the answer two thousand years ago, and it is still the answer today.

By His Stripes We Are Healed

"By his stripes we are healed." What a curious line, what a curious logic! One person gets lashed, another gets healed; one suffers, another is set free; one dies, another comes to life.

An odd logic, but a Gospel logic; Gospel not just because it appears in the Bible (see 1 Peter 2:24) but because it contains the kind of paradox that lies at the heart of the Good News of Jesus. Life comes from death and, sometimes, the death that produces life within us is not our own but the death of someone else.

How does this work? How can we be healed by someone else's suffering? Or, perhaps even more importantly, the reverse: How can we suffer so as to heal someone else?

This concept, vicarious suffering, has an important place within all the great religions of the world. That should tell us something. No spirituality worth the name does not, at some point, make a place for it. In Christianity, it lies at the heart of everything: Christ died so that we might live. By his stripes we are healed.

Now we have not always had the best explanation of how that works. Too often, both in theology and in spirituality, we took a metaphor too literally. For example, in theology, there was the idea that because of sin—original sin and our own sin—some great debt is owed to God, and the sufferings of Christ and of good people fill in that debt to the benefit of the rest of us. Scripture, on occasion, though not often, expresses this in metaphor. However, if this idea is taken literally, it does not do much justice to God. It makes God seem arbitrary, petty, and legalistic, and it gives the idea that there is, somewhere, a divine credit union within which sin and merits must be balanced like a bankbook. The idea is that sin makes a grace withdrawal, and sacrifice makes a grace deposit.

We had this idea in a popularized form within spirituality, although, admittedly, not in as crass a sense as just expressed. The idea was that good people could make sacrifices for others. Thus, for example, a good mother with a wayward son would make sacrifices for her son. She would do virtuous acts and "offer them up" for her son, and he would somehow be helped by that. By her stripes he was healed.

We want to be careful not to be too cynical about this. The logic behind this needs refinement, but both the sincerity of intention of the mother and the net result of her sacrifice should not be under-rated within the economy of grace. Her sacrifice *does* help her son, if he is at all open to grace. However, it helps him not because there is a divine credit union where her deposits of grace let him overdraw his account, so to speak, but because in the economy (perhaps not a good word here) of grace we are, indeed, helped by the sacrifice of others. How?

Let me illustrate with one simple example: Growing up as a young boy, I had a brother who was two years older than me. He was not only older chronologically, he was also considerably more mature. One Sunday afternoon, during a spring when I was eleven and he was thirteen, we were playing outside the house when we came upon a copper boiler that my mother had put there to catch water from the snow as it melted on a roof. There was a crust of ice over the water and, being a young boy, I wanted to break it. I picked up a small steel crowbar and was about to poke into the ice with it when my brother warned me: "Careful," he said, "if it slips you will ruin the boiler—its sides are soft." Then, seeing that I was going to do it anyway, he tried to wrench the steel bar away from me; but before he was able to, I slammed it into the ice…and, just as he had predicted, it glanced off the ice and punctured the side of the copper boiler, effectively ruining it.

The next morning at breakfast, my father, having seen the ruined boiler and having deduced the cause, confronted my brother and me at the table: "Who ruined that boiler?" Frightened and ashamed, but deeply aware of my guilt, I sat in silence, too immature to admit what I had done. After a brief pause, my brother spoke: "I did," he said, "I was trying to break the ice with a crowbar and it slipped and went through the side of the boiler." My father admonished him briefly, telling him that, at his age, he should have known better. He, for his part, did not protest that he did know better, nor did he look at me in anger, or gloat in glee. Mostly he just looked at me as a younger brother who was a bit immature and needed an older brother to bail him out.

He took the rap for me and, because of that, I grew up a bit. He suffered; I matured. By his stripes I was healed.

CHAPTER FIVE

The Resurrection—
Every Grave Opens Up!

The Resurrection and the Voice of Good Friday

Easter is about many things. We celebrate God's ultimate power to redeem death, sin, and injustice, but we also celebrate the now-glorified voices and wounds of the ones who died on other Good Fridays.

To this end, I would like to recount one such voice: that of an anonymous, young girl who was brutally raped and murdered by the Salvadoran military, at a place fittingly called La Cruz (the cross) in 1981. The story is reported by a journalist, Mark Danner. He describes how, after this particular massacre, some soldiers shared how one of their victims haunted them and how they could not get her out of their minds, long after her death.

The soldiers had plundered a village and raped many of the women. One of those was a young girl, an evangelical Christian, whom they had raped many times in a single afternoon and subsequently tortured. However, throughout this all, this young girl, clinging to her belief in Christ, had sung hymns:

> She had kept right on singing, too, even after they had done what had to be done, and shot her in the chest. She had lain there on La Cruz with the blood flowing from her chest,

and had kept on singing—a bit weaker than before, but still singing. And the soldiers, stupefied, had watched and pointed. Then they had grown tired of the game and shot her again, and she sang still, and their wonder began to turn to fear—until finally they had unsheathed their machetes and hacked her neck, and at last the singing had stopped.[8]

Gil Bailie, who makes this story a cornerstone in his monumental book on the cross and nonviolence, notes not just the remarkable similarity between her manner of death and Jesus's, but also the fact that, in both cases, part of the resurrection is that their voices live on. In Jesus's case, nobody witnessing his humiliating death on a lonely hillside, with his followers absent, would have predicted that this would be the most remembered death in history. The same is true for this young girl. Her rape and murder occurred in a very remote place, and all of those who might have wanted to immortalize her story were also killed. Yet her voice survives and will no doubt continue to grow in history, long after all those who violated her are forgotten.

As both Jesus and this young girl illustrate, powerlessness and anonymity, when linked to a heart that can sing the words "Forgive them for they know not what they do" while being humiliated and murdered, ultimately become their opposite: power and immortality. A death of this kind not only morally scars the conscience of its perpetrators and their sympathizers, it leaves something that can never be forgotten—a permanent echo that nobody will ever silence. What God raises after Good Friday is not only the body, but also the voice of the one who died.

A critic reviewing Danner's book in the *New York Times* tells how, after reading this story, he kept "straining hopelessly to hear the sound of that singing."

The task of Easter is to reenkindle the entire creed within ourselves. The earliest Christians, immediately after experiencing the resurrected Christ, spontaneously voiced a one-line creed: "Jesus is Lord!" That says it all. When we say that Jesus has been raised from the dead and is Lord of this world we are saying everything. We are saying that:

• God is ultimately still in charge of this universe, despite many indications to the contrary.

• Brutality and rape notwithstanding, at the end of the day, violence, injustice, and sin will be both silenced and overcome.

• Graciousness and gentleness, as manifested by Jesus, are ultimately what lies at the root of all of reality.

• This young girl, who was so brutally violated, has now been raised and lives, joyfully, in the heart of God.

• And her death, like Jesus's death, is redemptive precisely because, like him, she too, in the face of utter helplessness before the worst brutality our world contains, could still say, "Forgive them for they know not what they do."

To believe in the resurrection is to know that all of this is true. But the task of Easter asks still something else of us.

Easter asks us, as the critic in the *New York Times* so aptly put it, to strain to hear the sound of that girl's singing, to struggle to keep her, and her song, alive in our hearts. She is alive in God's heart, but we must keep her alive in ours as well.

Why? Not for sentimental reasons, nor simply because hers is an exceptional story. No. We must keep her alive in our hearts because her song is the leaven, the yeast of resurrection, which alone can raise up our own hearts so that we too might become exceptional. One of the tasks of Easter is to strain to hear the voice of Good Friday.

And the Atoms Moved!

Teilhard de Chardin was once asked by a critic, "What are you trying to do? Why all this talk about atoms and molecules when you are speaking about Jesus Christ?" He answered something to this effect: "I am trying to formulate a Christology that is large enough to incorporate Christ because Christ is not just an anthropological event but a cosmic phenomenon as well."

In essence, what he is saying is that Christ did not come just to reshape human history and save human beings, he came to reshape the earth and to save it as well.

That is a profound insight and it is nowhere more true than when we try to understand all that is implied in the resurrection of Christ. Jesus was raised from death to life. A dead body was resurrected and that has dimensions that are not just spiritual and psychological. There is something radically physical to this. When a dead body is brought to new life, the very physical structure of the universe is being rearranged—atoms and molecules are being changed. The resurrection is about more than just new hope being born in human consciousness.

The resurrection is the basis for human hope, surely. Without it, we could not hope for any future that includes our full humanity, beyond the rather limited and asphyxiating limits of this life. In the resurrection of Jesus we are given a new future; in it we are saved. But the resurrection gives a new future to the earth, the physical planet, as well. Christ came to save the earth, not just human beings, and his resurrection is also about the future of the earth.

The earth, like ourselves, needs saving. From what? For what?

In a proper Christian understanding of things, the earth is not just a stage for human beings; that is, a thing with no value in itself, apart from us. Like humanity, it too is God's work of art, God's child. In fact, it is the matrix from which we all spring. We are, in the end, only that part of God's creation that has become conscious of itself. Hence we do not stand apart from the earth and it does not exist simply for our benefit, like a stage for the actor, to be abandoned once the play is finished. Physical creation has value in itself, independent of humanity. We need to recognize that, and not just so that we practice better eco-ethics, so that the earth can continue to provide air, water, and food for future generations of human beings. We need to recognize the intrinsic value of the earth because ultimately it is Sister Earth, destined to share eternity with us.

But, like us, it is also subject to decay. Like us, it too is time-bound, mortal, and dying. Outside of an intervention from the outside, it has no future. Science has already, long ago, pointed out to us the law of entropy. Put simply, energy in our universe is running down. The sun is burning out. The years our earth has before it are, like the days of any human being, numbered, counted, finite. It will take some millions of years, but finitude is finitude. There will be an end to the earth as we know it, just as there will be an end to each of us as we know ourselves to be. Outside of something offered us from the outside we, both the earth and the humans living on it, have no future.

It is to this concept that the Epistle to the Romans refers when it tells us that creation, the physical cosmos, is subject to futility and that it is groaning and longing to be set free to enjoy the glorious liberty of the children of God. Romans then assures us that the earth will enjoy the same future as human beings (see Romans 8:18–23). In the resurrection it, too, is given a new possibility, transformation, and an eternal future. How will it be redeemed? Just as we are redeemed, through the resurrection of Jesus. The resurrection brings into our world, both into its spiritual and its physical elements, a new power, a new arrangement of things, a new hope: something so radical (and physical) that it can only be compared to what happened at the initial creation. In the beginning, the atoms and the molecules of this universe were made out of nothing, nature took its shape, and its reality and laws shaped everything from then on until the resurrection of Jesus. Something new happened then; and that event, that physical event, touched every aspect of the universe, from the soul and psyche in every man and woman to the inner core of every atom and molecule.

In the resurrection of Jesus, the very atoms of the universe were rearranged. Teilhard is right. The resurrection is not just about people, it is about the future of the planet as well.

And Forgiveness Poured Out

The world contains only one thing that is truly novel: forgiveness. And this is the message of the resurrection. Everything else is like the words of an old song repeating itself endlessly over and over again. There is normally only one song that gets sung: the song of betrayal, hurt, resentment, and non-forgiveness. That pattern never changes. There is an unbroken chain of unforgiveness, resentment, and anger stretching back to Adam and Eve.

We are all part of that chain. Everyone is wounded and everyone wounds. Everyone sins and everyone is sinned against. Everyone needs to forgive and everyone needs to be forgiven.

Betrayal is an archetypal structure within the human soul, just as sin is innate within the human condition. We, all of us, betray and sin. We betray ourselves, betray our loved ones, betray our communities, and we sin against our God. Everyone stands in need of forgiveness.

But we are also, each one of us, betrayed and sinned against. We are betrayed by our loved ones, by churches, by our communities, and, in a manner of speaking, we are betrayed even by our God. It is not for nothing that, on the cross, Jesus, incarnating there all that is human, cries out: "My God, my God, why have you forsaken me?" (Matthew 27:46). We all feel betrayed at that deep level sometimes. Hence, as badly as we need to be forgiven, we also need to forgive.

We have hurt others and we have been hurt. We have sinned and we have been sinned against. When we wake up to this reality, we have a choice. Like Judas we can cleanse ourselves, figuratively speaking, by taking what we have gained by our sin—the thirty pieces of silver—throwing it back into the Temple and walking away; purified, but unforgiven, walking straight toward suicide. Conversely, though, we can do what Peter did after his great betrayal: weep bitterly and then return, humbled, compromised, and scarred, but forgiven, and walk solidly back into life. In forgiveness lies the difference between the choice for suicide and the choice for life.

But forgiveness is not easy. An old adage says: "To err is human, to forgive is divine." More accurately, one might put it this way: *To forgive is the grace that is given by the resurrection.*

The resurrection of Jesus has many dimensions. At one level, it was a physical event. The dead body of Jesus was raised, the cosmic universe at its deepest level suddenly had a new set of laws, and the very atoms of this universe, as nature first arranged them, were rearranged. Something radically new, physically new, as radical and new as the original creation, appeared within history. This aspect should never be, as it recently has been, understated.

However, the resurrection was also a spiritual event and that, too, is important. In the resurrection of Jesus we are given not just the potential for a resurrected body and a resurrected cosmos, we are given as well the possibility of forgiveness—of being forgiven and of forgiving each other. That new possibility and its radical novelty also should never be understated. From the beginning of time until Jesus's resurrection, dead bodies stayed dead. And from Adam and Eve until that same resurrection, wounded and dead hearts stayed wounded and dead. All that now has changed. There are new possibilities.

What is new in the resurrection is not just the unbelievable new possibility of physical resurrection. The resurrection gives us, too, the equally unbelievable possibility of the newness of life that forgiving and being forgiven brings. In our day-to-day lives, that is how we are asked to appropriate the resurrection of Jesus: by forgiving and by letting ourselves be forgiven.

In Mark's account of the death and resurrection, our human condition is symbolized by a young man who was following Jesus's journey to the cross from a safe distance. At a certain point this young man, who is wearing only a white linen cloth, is seized. He escapes his captors and flees naked, leaving the cloth behind (see Mark 14:51–52). That betrayal is yours and mine. But we next meet him on Easter Sunday, sitting on the tomb of the resurrected Jesus, wearing again his linen cloth and announcing to the whole world that Jesus has been raised, that an unbelievable newness has burst into our world, and that there is something even beyond our wounds, sins, and betrayals. The chain of anger has been broken.

And God Has the Last Word

Theologians sometimes try to simplify the meaning of the resurrection by packaging its essence into one sentence: In the resurrection, God vindicated Jesus: his life, his message, and his fidelity. What does that mean?

Jesus entered our world preaching faith, love, and forgiveness, but the world didn't accept that. Instead it crucified him and, in that crucifixion, seemingly shamed his message. We see this most clearly on the cross when Jesus is taunted, mocked, and challenged: "If you are the Son of God, come down from there!" "If your message is true, let God verify that right now!" "If your fidelity is more than plain stubbornness and human ignorance, then why are you dying in shame?" (see Matthew 27:27–44).

And what was God's response to those taunts? Nothing. No commentary, no defense, no apologia, no counter-challenge; just silence. Jesus dies in silence. Neither he nor the God he believed in tried to fill that excruciating void with any consoling words or explanations that would challenge people to look at the bigger picture or the brighter side of things. None of that. Just silence.

Jesus died in silence—inside God's silence and inside the world's incomprehension. And we can let ourselves be humbly scandalized by that silence, just as we can let ourselves be perpetually scandalized by the seeming triumph of evil, pain, and suffering in our world. God's silence can forever scandalize us: in the Jewish holocaust, in ethnic genocides, in brutal and senseless wars, in the earthquakes and tsunamis which kill thousands of people and devastate whole countries, in the deaths of countless people taken out of this life by cancer and by violence, in how unfair life can be sometimes, and in the casual manner that those without conscience can rape whole areas of life seemingly without consequence. Where is God in all of this? What's God's answer?

God's answer is in the resurrection—in the resurrection of Jesus and in the perennial resurrection of goodness within life itself. But resurrection is not necessarily rescue. God doesn't necessarily rescue us from the effects of evil, or even from death. Evil does what it does, natural disasters are what they are, and those without conscience can rape even as they feed off life's sacred fire. God doesn't intervene. The parting of the Red Sea isn't a weekly occurrence. God lets his loved ones suffer and die, just as Jesus let his dear friend Lazarus die and just as God let Jesus die. God redeems; God raises us up afterward in a deeper, more lasting vindication. And the truth of that statement can be tested empirically.

Despite every appearance, sometimes, in the end, love does triumph over hatred. Peace does triumph over chaos. Forgiveness does triumph over bitterness. Hope does triumph over cynicism. Fidelity does triumph over despair. Virtue does triumph over sin. Conscience does triumph over callousness. Life does triumph over death. And good does triumph over evil, always. Remember, as Mohandas K. Gandhi, who was quoted before, wrote: "There have been murderers and tyrants, and for a time they can seem invincible. But in the end they always fall." [9]

The resurrection, most forcibly, makes that point. God has the last word. The resurrection of Jesus is that last word. From the ashes of shame, of seeming defeat, failure, and death, a new, deeper, and eternal life perennially bursts forth. Our faith begins at the very point where it seems it might end, in God's seeming silence at Jesus's death.

And what does this ask of us?

First of all, simply that we trust its truth. The resurrection of Jesus asks us to believe what Gandhi affirmed, namely, that in the end evil will not have the last word. It will fall. Good will eventually triumph.

More deeply, it asks us to roll the dice of our lives on that trust and on that truth. What Jesus taught is true. Virtue is not naïve, even when it is shamed. Sin and cynicism are naïve, even when they appear to triumph. Those who genuflect before God and others in conscience will find meaning and joy, even when they are deprived of the world's pleasures. Those who drink in and manipulate sacred energy without conscience will not find meaning and life, even when they taste pleasure. Those who live in honesty, no matter the cost, will find freedom. Those who lie and rationalize will find themselves imprisoned in self-hate. Those who live in trust will find love. God's silence can be trusted, even when we die inside of it.

We can live in faith, love, forgiveness, conscience, and fidelity in spite of everything that suggests that they aren't true. They will bring us to what is deepest inside of life and love, because God vindicates virtue. God vindicates love. God vindicates conscience. God vindicates forgiveness. God vindicates fidelity. God vindicated Jesus and will vindicate us if we remain faithful as Jesus did.

A String of Empty Tombs

Spring and Easter: a conspiracy between nature and religion, creation and redemption, to make newness, to thaw things out, to rejuvenate and re-virginize, to make sunshine, to warm frozen places, and to produce new buds on the trees and new enthusiasm in the heart! It's the season of the resurrection. At the end of winter, sometime after the first equinox, God is hard at it, melting earth and melting hearts.

We celebrate many things with Easter. The resurrection is not just the mystery of Christ rising from the dead and of our future rising from the dead. It's life's spring—the event and power that brings new life out of what's been crucified by winter, from what's died, from what lies frozen and lifeless. Like nature needs spring each year, so, too, we need regular resurrections. Much in us lies frozen, crucified, lifeless. It is possible to be dead and not know it, to be asleep and still think we are awake, to be bitter as a slave and still think we are loving.

Physical death, for most of us, comes last. First, there is the long series of other deaths, of crucifixions, of diminishments and losses. In this, too, we follow the pattern of what happened in Christ. Christ came as God's perfect image, the most precious, most sensitive, most special human being ever. It was that, the uniqueness and goodness, which was crucified. And this perfect image still gets crucified, in us. It is precisely in those areas of our lives where we bear God's image the most perfectly, where we are most precious, most sensitive and most special, that, invariably, we get crucified. What's calloused, tough, and homogenized, survives, living on, helping us go through the motions of life: our automatic pilot in death. But what is most precious in us ends up in a tomb: a dream crucified, a Christ entombed, a winter set in, a human being frozen over. Before being buried in our graves we are, largely, buried in our lives.

Mainly because of this, we begin to sin. Our infidelities, our lack of gratitude, our lack of prayer, our propensity to misunderstand and to hurt each other, our need to lie and rationalize, and our excessive self-preoccupations, occur mostly because what's best in us, the image of God, lies frozen and lifeless inside us. Our poverty and bitterness come from that. And so we begin to settle for second best. We make do: a life without enthusiasm, without fire, with passion quieted, with joy frozen. We despair, not by suicide, but by protest, protesting that our lives are without new possibilities: "If you really knew what my life is like, you wouldn't tell me I could be happy!" Eventually, hope fades into agnosticism. Agnosticism invariably turns to despair. Bitterly, we accept our limits: "This is the way I am, this is the way things are, this is the way it has always been. This is the way it will always be!" Nothing can surprise us anymore. We know what is possible for us, and what is possible in no way approximates our dreams.

So we live on, far from fully alive, on automatic pilot, the Christ in us lying in the tomb, what's most precious in us frozen under bitterness. There is darkness at the end of the tunnel, save for one thing: spring and resurrection! Every spring, a warm sun reappears, and nature and we are given the opportunity to unthaw, to resurrect. Some years back, I received an Easter card which contained only these simple words: "May you leave behind you a string of empty tombs!" That's the challenge of Easter: To resurrect daily, to leave behind us a string of empty tombs, to let our crucified hopes and dreams be resurrected so that, like Christ, our lives will radiate the truth that, in the end, everything is good, reality can be trusted. Love does triumph over apathy and hatred, togetherness over loneliness, peace over chaos, and forgiveness over bitterness. We need regular resurrections. Spring and the resurrection are the season to let ourselves be unthawed, to re-virginize, to come to second naiveté, to think young again, to give the child in us scope again, to be open again to new possibilities, to surprise, to a new frolic under the sun after a cold bitter time.

Nature—all of it, including ourselves—is incredibly resilient, incredibly resurrectable. Given any chance, life wins out, brokenness heals, bitterness melts, new seeds form and life bursts forth from what once appeared to be dead. Crucifixions, bitterness, and winters will come, but spring and resurrection are arsonists, both of them.

May we all leave behind us a string of empty tombs.

Seeing the Resurrection

In my mid-twenties, I spent a year as a student at the University of San Francisco. I had just been ordained a priest and was finishing off a graduate degree in theology. Easter Sunday that year was a gorgeous, sunny, spring day, but it didn't find me in a sunny mood. I was a long way from home, away from my family and my community, homesick, and alone. Virtually all the friends that I had developed during that year of studies—other graduate students in theology—were gone, celebrating Easter with their own families. I was homesick and alone and, beyond that, I nursed the usual heartaches and obsessions of the young and restless. My mood was far from spring and Easter.

I went for a walk that afternoon and the spring air, the sun, and the fact that it was Easter did little to cheer me up; if anything they helped catalyze a deeper sense of aloneness. But there are different ways of waking up. As Leonard Cohen says, There's a crack in everything and that's where the light gets in. I needed a little awakening and it was provided. At a point, I saw a beggar sitting at the entrance to a park with a sign in front of him that read: "It is springtime and I am blind!" The irony wasn't lost on me: I was as blind as he was! With what I was seeing, it might as well have been a cold, rainy Good Friday. Sunshine, spring, and Easter were being wasted on me.

It was a moment of grace, and I have recalled that encounter many times since, but it didn't alter my mood at the time. I continued my walk, restless as before, and eventually went home for dinner. During that year of studies, I was a live-in chaplain at a convent that had a youth hostel attached to it, and the rule of the house was that the chaplain was to eat by himself, in his own private dining room. So, even though that wasn't exactly what a doctor would order for a restless and homesick young man, I had a private dinner that Easter Sunday.

But the resurrection did arrive for me on that Easter Sunday, albeit a bit late in the day: Two other graduate students and I had made plans to meet on the beach at nightfall, light a large fire, and celebrate our own version of the Easter Vigil. So, just before dark, I caught a bus to the beach and met my friends, a nun and priest. We lit a large bonfire (still legal in those days), sat around it for several hours, and ended up confessing to each other that we'd each had a miserable Easter. That fire did for us what the blessing of the fire the evening before at the Easter Vigil hadn't done. It renewed in us a sense of the energy and newness that lie at the heart of life. As we watched the fire and talked, of everything and nothing, my mood began to shift, my restlessness quieted, and the heaviness lifted. I began to sense spring and Easter.

In John's Gospel account of the resurrection, he tells the story of how on the morning of the first Easter, the Beloved Disciple runs to the tomb where Jesus has been buried and peers into it. He sees that it is empty and that all that's left there are the clothes, neatly folded, within which Jesus's body had been wrapped. And, because he is a disciple who sees with the eyes of love, he understands what all this means: He grasps the resurrection and knows that Jesus has risen. He sees spring. He understands with his eyes.

Hugo of St. Victor once famously said: "Love is the eye." When we see with love we not only see straight and clearly, we also see depth and meaning. The reverse is also true. It is not for some arbitrary reason that after Jesus rose from the dead some could see him and others could not. Love is the eye. Those searching for life through the eyes of love, like Mary of Magdala searching for Jesus in the garden on Easter Sunday morning, see spring and the resurrection. Any other kind of eye, and we're blind in springtime.

When I took my walk that Easter afternoon all those years ago in San Francisco, I wasn't exactly Mary of Magdala looking for Jesus in a garden, nor the Beloved Disciple fired by love running off to look into the tomb of Jesus. In my youthful restlessness, I was looking for myself and meeting only my anxious self. And that's a kind of blindness.

Without the eyes of love we're blind, to both spring and the resurrection. I learned that theological lesson, not in a church or a classroom, but on a lonely, restless Easter Sunday in San Francisco when I ran into a blind beggar.

Midwifing the Resurrection

It's no accident that when Jesus rose from the dead he appeared first to women. Why? During his pre-resurrection ministry, or at least it seems, he called mainly men to be the principal actors. Why a certain reversal at the resurrection?

We can only speculate, but one reason might be that women are midwives. Something new is being born in the resurrection, and women are the ones who attend to birth.

That's a metaphor worth reflecting on; not just in terms of the importance of women in ministry, but especially in terms of how we are all, women and men alike, called to respond to the resurrection: namely, by becoming midwives of hope and trust. And it's a needed vocation because all of us, perpetually, are in the agony of struggling to give birth to trust. Why?

Because we've all been wounded by betrayal, abuse, broken promises, broken relationships, and empty words. By the time we reach adulthood, there is enough disillusionment in us to make it natural to say: "Why should I trust you? Why should I believe this? Why is anything different this time? I know how empty words can be!" The older we get, the harder it is to trust and the easier it is to become skeptical and cynical.

Yet none of us wants to be this way. Something inside us wants to trust, to hope, to believe in the goodness of things, to again feel that trustful enthusiasm we once had as children, when we were innocent (and *innocent* means "unwounded"), and when we could still take another's hand in trust. No one wants to be outside the circle of trust.

But it's a struggle, an agony of sorts, as we know. We'd like to trust, but often we can't give birth to it. That's where a midwife can be helpful.

When a baby is born, normally the head pushes its way through the birth canal first, opening the way for the body to follow. A good midwife can be very helpful at this time, doing everything from giving support, through giving reassurance, through giving instruction, through teaching us how to breathe, through actively helping to pull the new life through the birth canal. Her help can sometimes mean the difference between life and death, and it always makes the birth easier and healthier.

That's true too for trust and hope. A good midwife can be helpful in bringing these to birth. What can she bring that's helpful? Insight, support, reassurance, certain spiritual "breathing exercises," and experienced hands that can, if necessary, help pull the new child through the birth canal.

And one of the things a midwife of hope needs to do is what Jesus did when he met people, women and men alike, after his resurrection. He sent them back to "Galilee" where he promised they would refind their hope and trust. What is "Galilee"?

In the Gospels, "Galilee" is more than a geographical place. It's a place of the heart: the place of falling in love, of first fervor, of being inflamed with high ideals, of walking on water because one is naïve and trustful enough to believe that this is possible. "Galilee" is the place we were before our hearts and ideals got crucified, the place inside us where trust and hope are gestated.

A good midwife of hope, like Jesus on the morning of the resurrection, invites people to "Galilee." How? Here's an example: The famed American educator Allan Bloom tells a story of how a particular distasteful incident in a classroom once helped change forever the way he teaches. Sitting in a lecture hall as an undergraduate, he felt assaulted by a professor who began his class with words to this effect: *You come here with your small-town, parochial biases, your naïveté. Well, I'm going to bathe you in great truth and set you free!*

Bloom remarks how this reminded him of a boy who had very solemnly informed him when he was seven that there was no Santa Claus or Easter Bunny. This was no great truth, just an invitation to cynicism, like the professor's comment. Reflecting on this, Bloom resolved to forever teach in exactly the opposite way. He would begin his classes this way: *You come here with your many experiences and your sophistication; well, I respect that, but I'm going to try to teach you how to believe in Santa Claus and the Easter Bunny again—and then maybe you'll have some chance to be happy!*

The resurrection of Jesus is about more than believing in Santa and the Easter Bunny; but, even so, Bloom's pedagogy tells us something about what it means to go back to "Galilee" and give birth to trust in our lives.

Somewhere in life we lose the child in us and lose too the trust and hope that go with that. It's a painful struggle to give birth to trust again and, in that struggle, a midwife of hope, someone who believes in the resurrection, can indeed be a wonderful friend.

Waiting for the Resurrection

We live in difficult times. We've only to watch the news on any given evening. If there's an all-knowing, all-powerful, and all-loving God who's Lord of this universe, his presence isn't very evident on the evening news. There's violence all over the planet, fueled on every side by self-righteous ideologies that sanction hatred, by self-interest that lets communities fend for themselves, and by a socially approved greed that lets the poor fend for themselves.

It's fair and reflective to wonder: Where is the resurrection in all of this? Why is God seemingly so inactive? Where is the vindication of Easter Sunday?

These are important questions, even if they aren't particularly deep or new. They were the questions used to taunt Jesus on the cross: "If you're the Son of God, come down off that cross! If you're God, prove it! Act now!" (see Matthew 27:27–44). Then and now, it seems, we've never figured out why salvation can't work like a normal movie where, at the end, a morally superior violence kills off all that's bad.

Except God doesn't work like a Hollywood movie and never has. For centuries people prayed for a messiah, a superman, to come and display a power and a glory that would overpower evil; but what they got was a helpless baby lying in the straw. And when that baby grew up, they wanted him to overthrow the Roman Empire; instead, he let himself be crucified. We haven't changed much in what we expect of God.

But God, as revealed in the death and resurrection of Jesus, doesn't meet our expectations even as he infinitely exceeds them. What the resurrection teaches is that God doesn't forcibly intervene to stop pain and death. Instead he redeems the pain and vindicates the death. God rids the world of evil not by using force to blot it out, but by vindicating what's good in the eyes of evil so that eventually the good is all that's left. Evil has to forever "look on the one whom they have pierced" (John 19:37) until it understands what it has done and lets itself be transformed. How does this work?

What the resurrection of Jesus reveals is that there's a deep moral structure to the universe, that the contours of the universe are love and goodness and truth, and that this structure, anchored at its center by Ultimate Love and Power, is nonnegotiable: You live life its way or it simply won't come out right. More importantly, the reverse is also true: If you respect the structure and live life its way, what's good and true and loving will eventually triumph, always, despite everything. If this is true, and it is, then we don't have to escape pain and death to achieve victory—we've only to remain faithful, good, and true inside of them.

However, part of what's revealed here is that we need a great patience, a patience called hope. God's day will come, but God, it seems, is not in any hurry.

Good and truth will always triumph, but this triumph must be waited for, not because God wants us to endure pain as some kind of test, but because God, unlike ourselves, doesn't use coercion or violence to achieve an aim. God uses only love, truth, beauty, and goodness, and God uses these by embedding them, structurally and nonnegotiably, into the universe itself, like a giant moral immune system that eventually, always, brings the body back to health. God doesn't need to intervene like a superhero at the end of a Hollywood movie, one who uses a morally superior violence to kill the bad people so that the good are spared pain and death. God lets the universe right itself the way a body does when it is attacked by a virus. The immune system eventually does its work, even if, in the short term, there is pain and infection. Always, in the end, the universe rights itself.

Simply put: Whenever we do anything wrong, anything at all, it won't turn out right. It can't. The structure of the universe won't receive it and it comes back to us, one way or the other. Conversely, whenever we do something right—anything that's true, good, loving, or beautiful—the universe vindicates that. It judges our every act, and its judgment allows no exceptions.

Perhaps that judgment isn't immediate: It can seem a long time in coming and thus, for a time, we can be confused and ask, "Why doesn't God, truth, and goodness, come down off the cross?" But eventually, always, and without a single exception, as Gandhi says, evil is shamed and good triumphs. The resurrection works.

Living beyond our Crucifixions

Every dream eventually gets crucified. How? By time, circumstance, jealousy, and that curious, perverse dictate, somehow innate within the order of things, that ensures that there is always someone or something that cannot leave well enough alone, but, for reasons of its own, must hunt down and strike what is good. The good will always be envied, hated, pursued, smudged, killed. That's true even of dreams. Something there is that needs a crucifixion. Every "body" of Christ inevitably suffers the same fate as Jesus. There's no smooth ride for what's whole, good, true, or beautiful.

But that's only half the equation—the bad half. What's also true, what the resurrection teaches, is that, while nothing that is of God can avoid crucifixion, no "body" of Christ ever stays in the tomb for long either. God always rolls back the stone and, soon enough, new life bursts forth and we see why that original life had to be crucified. ("Wasn't it necessary that the Christ should so have to suffer and die?" [see Luke 24:26]) Resurrection follows crucifixion. Every crucified body will rise again.

But where do we meet the resurrection? Where does the resurrected Christ meet us?

Scripture is subtle, but clear. Where can we expect to meet the resurrected Christ after a crucifixion? The Gospel tell us that, on the morning of the resurrection, the female followers of Jesus, the midwives of hope, set out for the tomb of Jesus, carrying spices, intending to anoint and embalm a dead body. Well-intentioned but misguided, what they find is not a dead body, but an empty tomb and an angel challenging them with these words: "Why are you looking for the living among the dead? Go instead into Galilee and you will find him there!" (see Matthew 28:1–10).

"Go instead into Galilee." What a curious expression! What is Galilee? Why go back? In the post-resurrection accounts in the Gospels, Galilee is not simply a physical geography. It is, first of all, a place in the heart. Galilee is the dream, the road of discipleship that they had once walked with Jesus, and that place and time when their hearts had most burned with hope and enthusiasm. And now, just when they feel that this all is dead, that their faith is only fantasy, they are told to go back to the place where it all began: "Go back to Galilee. He will meet you there!"

And they do go back, to Galilee, to that special place in their hearts, to the dream, to their discipleship. Sure enough, Jesus appears to them there. He doesn't appear exactly as they remember him, or as often as they would like him to, but he does appear as more than a ghost or a mere idea. The Christ that appears to them after the resurrection no longer fits their original expectation, but he is physical enough to eat fish in their presence, real enough to be touched as a human being, and powerful enough to change their lives forever.

Ultimately, that is what the resurrection challenges us to do: to go back to Galilee, to return to the dream, hope, and discipleship that had once inflamed us but that now is crucified.

This, too, is what it means to "be on the road to Emmaus." In Luke's Gospel, we are told that on the day of the resurrection, two disciples were walking away from Jerusalem toward Emmaus, their faces downcast. That single line contains an entire spirituality: For Luke, Jerusalem (like Galilee for the other Gospel writers) means the dream, the hope, the kingdom, the center from which all is to begin and where ultimately all is to culminate. And the disciples are "walking away" from this, away from the dream, toward Emmaus. Emmaus was a Roman spa—a Las Vegas or Monte Carlo of human consolation. Their dream has been crucified and the disciples, discouraged and hope-emptied, are walking away from Jerusalem and toward human consolation, muttering: "But we had hoped!"

They never get to Emmaus. Jesus appears to them on the road, reshapes their hope in the light of the crucifixion, and turns them back toward Jerusalem (see Luke 24:13–35).

One of the essential messages of Easter is this: Whenever we are discouraged in our faith, whenever our hopes seem to be crucified, we need to go back to Galilee and Jerusalem, that is, to the dream, to the road of discipleship that we had embarked upon before everything went wrong. The temptation, of course, whenever we feel this way, whenever the kingdom doesn't seem to work, is to abandon discipleship for human consolation, to set out instead for Emmaus, for the consolation of Las Vegas and Monte Carlo.

But, as we already know, we never quite get to Emmaus. In one guise or another, Christ always meets us on the road, burns holes in our hearts, explains the latest crucifixion to us, and sends us back—to Galilee, to Jerusalem, and to our abandoned discipleship. Once there, it all makes sense again.

Daily Resurrection

Gilbert K. Chesterton once wrote a poem he titled "A Second Childhood." It speaks of the resurrection:

When all my days are ending
And I have no song to sing,
I think that I shall not be too old
To stare at everything;

As I stared once at a nursery door
Or a tall tree and a swing.

…

Men grow too old for love, my love,
Men grow too old for lies;
But I shall not grow too old to see
Enormous night arise,
A cloud that is larger than the world
And a monster made of eyes.

…

Men grow too old to woo, my love,
Men grow too old to wed;
But I shall not grow too old to see
Hung crazily overhead
Incredible rafters when I wake
And I find that I am not dead.

…

Strange crawling carpets of the grass,
Wide windows of the sky;
So in this perilous grace of God
With all my sins go I:
And things grow new though I grow old,
Though I grow old and die.[10]

What the resurrection of Jesus promises is that things can always be new again. It's never too late to start over. Nothing is irrevocable. No betrayal is final. No sin is unforgivable. Every form of death can be overcome. There isn't any loss that can't be redeemed. Every day is virgin. There is really no such thing as old age.

In the resurrection we are assured that there are no doors that are eternally closed: Every time we close a door or one is closed upon us,

God opens another for us. The resurrection assures us that God never gives up on us, even if we give up on ourselves, that God writes straight with the crooked lines of our lives, that we can forever re-virginize, regain lost innocence, become post-sophisticated, and move beyond bitterness. In a scheme of things where Jesus breathes out forgiveness on those who betray him and God raises dead bodies, we can begin to believe that in the end, as Julian of Norwich puts it, "all will be well... and every manner of being will be well." Everything, including our own lives, eventually will end sunny-side up.

However, the challenge of living this out is not just that of believing that Jesus rose physically from the grave, but also, and perhaps even more importantly, to believe that—no matter our age, mistakes, betrayals, wounds, and deaths—we can begin each day afresh, virgin, innocent again, a child, a moral infant, stunned at the newness of it all. No matter what we've done, our future is forever pregnant with wonderful new possibility. Resurrection is not just a question of one day, after death, rising from the dead, but it is also about daily rising from the many mini-graves within which we so often find ourselves.

How does belief in the resurrection help us rise from these mini-graves? By keeping us open to surprise, newness, and freshness in our lives. Not an easy thing to do. We are human and we cannot avoid falling into depression, bitterness, sin, betrayal, cynicism, and the tiredness that comes with age. Like Jesus, we too will have our crucifixions. More than one grave awaits us. Yet our faith in the resurrection invites us precisely to live beyond these. As John Shea so aptly put it: What the resurrection teaches us is not how to live, but how to live again, and again, and again!

G.K. Chesterton, whom we quoted earlier, was also fond of saying: Learn to look at things familiar until they look unfamiliar again.

Familiarity is the greatest of all illusions.[11] In essence, that captures one of the real challenges of believing in the resurrection. If the resurrection is to have power in our lives, we must give up the illusion of familiarity, particularly as this pertains to all that's nearest to us, because the most common cancer that eats away at our marriages, families, communities, friendships, and simply at the joy we might have in living, is precisely the cancer of familiarity. We think we know, we think we understand, we think we have things figured out, and we end up psyching-out life and each other, leaving them no room for newness, for surprise, for the unfamiliar, for the resurrection.

Familiarity breeds contempt. Nothing robs us of joy more than that, and nothing destroys our marriages, families, communities, and friendships more than a contemptuousness that is born of familiarity. The resurrection tells us that familiarity is an illusion—the greatest of all illusions. The resurrection invites us to look at things familiar until they look unfamiliar again because, in the end, a startling, delightful surprise is hidden in all that is familiar.

I Believe in the Resurrection

To believe in the resurrection of Jesus is to be comforted, comforted at a level so deep that nothing in life is ultimately a threat any longer. In the resurrection, the hand of God soothes us and the voice of God assures us, frightened children that we are, that all is good and that all will remain good forever and ever.

The resurrection is not just something that happened to Jesus two thousand years ago and will happen to each of us sometime in the future, after we die, when our own bodies will be raised to new life. It is that, but it is much more. The resurrection is something that buoys up every moment of life and every aspect of reality. God is always making new life and undergirding it with a goodness, graciousness, mercy, and love that, in the end, heals all wounds, forgives all sins, and brings deadness of all kinds to new life.

We feel this resurrecting power in the most ordinary moments of our lives. A sense of the resurrection, understood in its deepest sense, manifests itself unconsciously in our vitality, in what we call health, in the feeling, however dimly it is sensed, that it is good to be alive. Allow me an illustration here:

The sociologist of religion Peter Berger, outlining what he calls "rumors of angels in everyday life," gives us the following reflection:

> Consider the most ordinary, and probably the most funda-
> mental of all—the ordinary gesture by which a mother
> reassures her anxious child. A child wakes up in the night,
> perhaps from a bad dream and finds himself surrounded by
> darkness, alone, beset by nameless threats. At such a moment
> the contours of trusted reality are blurred and invisible, in the
> terror of incipient chaos the child cries out for his mother.
> It is hardly an exaggeration to say that, at this moment, the
> mother is being invoked as a high priestess of protective
> order. It is she (and, in many cases, she alone) who has the
> power to banish the chaos and to restore the benign shape of
> the world. And, of course, any good mother will do just that.
> She will take the child and cradle him in the timeless gesture
> of the Magna Mater who became our Madonna. She will
> turn on a lamp, perhaps, which will encircle the scene with
> a warm glow of reassuring light. She will speak or sing to
> the child and the content of this communication will invari-
> ably be the same—"Don't be afraid— everything is in order,
> everything is all right."[12]

The mother's comforting reassurance, "Don't be afraid; it is all right," is, in fact, a profession of faith in God and the resurrection. When she says these words, she is making an act of faith just as surely, even if not as explicitly, as if she were saying: "I believe in God, the Father Almighty...and I believe in the resurrection of the body and life everlasting."

When she assures the child that there is nothing to be frightened about, she means it, and she means it (without her even realizing it) not so much on the basis that there are no immediate dangers to the child or because she is herself able to protect the child as on the basis that, ultimately, everything is all right. What she senses that makes her able to comfort the child is that there is nothing to be afraid of, even if something should kill us or if we should kill ourselves, because at the deepest level we are all in the hands of graciousness and love, not in the hands of maliciousness and terror. To say: "Don't be afraid," and mean it is to say that, in the end, the power of goodness is stronger than the power of malice, that dead bodies come out of graves, that all our mistakes will be forgiven, and that all terrors are phantom.

That is the power of the resurrection! That is what we mean when we say: "I believe in the resurrection of the body and life everlasting." The resurrection means more than just the fact that God raised the body of Jesus from the dead. It means that God's power to raise death to life buoys up every moment of life and every aspect of reality. The very atomic structure of the cosmos feels and knows that resurrecting power. That is why it (like us, when we are healthy) pushes forward blindly, buoyed up by a hope that it cannot understand.

Do you want to understand the power of the resurrection? Meditate on Michelangelo's *Pietà*: A woman holds a dead body in her arms, but everything about her and about the scene itself says loudly and clearly: "Don't be afraid. It's all right. Everything is and will be all right!"

ACKNOWLEDGMENTS

I need to thank many people for their help in writing this book. The biggest debt of gratitude goes to Alicia von Stamwitz, literary mentor and literary editor, who asked me to write this book and helped steer me through its birth. A deep thanks to Mark Lombard and everyone else at Franciscan Media for their faith in me. Thanks too to John R. Donahue, S.J., whose commentaries on Mark's Gospel were, for me, a "Da Vinci Code" that helped unravel part of the secret of the cross. I want to thank too my colleagues at Oblate School of Theology in San Antonio, Texas, for their constant intellectual challenge. Finally, a thank-you to my two families, the Rolheisers and the Oblates of Mary Immaculate, who keep me housed, clothed, fed, warm, loved, and, not least, chaperoned. I write with a great deal of support and a great deal of gratitude.

NOTES

1. Nikos Kazantzakis, *Saint Francis* (New York: Simon and Schuster, 1962), 139.

2. Theodore Roethke, "In A Dark Time," in *The Rag and Bone Shop of the Heart: A Poetry Anthology*, edited by Bly, Hillman, and Meade (New York: HarperPerennial, 1993), 22.

3. David Van Biema, "Why Did Jesus Have to Die?" *TIME* (April 12, 2004): 45–51.

4. C.H. Dodd, *Benefits of His Passion* (Nashville: Abingdon, 1956), 16–17.

5. Thomas Keating, quoted in an interview with Betty Sue Flowers in *Heartfulness: Transformation in Christ* (Butler, NJ: Contemplative Outreach, 2010), 116–117.

6. Mohandas K. Gandhi, quoted by Megan McKenna in *The New Stations of the Cross: The Way of the Cross According to Scripture* (New York: Image, 2003), 39.

7. Rainer Maria Rilke, "Sonnets to Orpheus IV," in *The Rag and Bone Shop of the Heart,* 100.

8. Mark Danner, *The Massacre at El Mozote* (New York: Vintage, 1994), 78–79.

9. Gandhi, in McKenna, *New Stations.*

10. Gilbert Keith Chesterton, "Second Childhood," *The Ballad of St. Barbara, and Other Verses.* Available at http://www.gutenberg.org/files/32167/32167-h/32167-h.htm.

11. Gilbert Keith Chesterton, *Everlasting Man.* Available at http://gutenberg.net.au/ebooks01/0100311.txt.

12. Peter L. Berger, *A Rumor of Angels: Modern Society and the Rediscovery of the Supernatural* (New York: Doubleday, 1969), 57ff.

ALSO BY RONALD ROLHEISER

Books

Against an Infinite Horizon: The Finger of God in Our Everyday Lives
(New York: Crossroad, 2002)

Forgotten Among the Lilies: Learning to Love Beyond Our Fears (New
York: Image, 2007)

The Holy Longing: The Search for a Christian Spirituality (New York:
Doubleday, 1999)

Our One Great Act of Fidelity: Waiting for Christ in the Eucharist (New
York: Image, 2011)

Prayer: Our Deepest Longing (Cincinnati: Franciscan Media, 2013)

The Restless Heart: Finding Our Spiritual Home in Times of Loneliness
(New York: Doubleday, 2004)

Sacred Fire: A Vision for a Deeper Human and Christian Maturity (New
York: Image, 2014)

The Shattered Lantern: Rediscovering a Felt Presence of God (New York:
Crossroad, 2005)

Audio

Against an Infinite Horizon: The Finger of God in Our Everyday Lives
(Cincinnati: Franciscan Media, 2003)

Forgotten Among the Lilies: Learning to Love Beyond Our Fears
(Cincinnati: Franciscan Media, 2005)

The Holy Longing: The Search for a Christian Spirituality (Cincinnati:
Franciscan Media, 2003)

Our One Great Act of Fidelity: Waiting for Christ in the Eucharist
(Cincinnati: Franciscan Media, 2013)

The Restless Heart: Finding Our Spiritual Home in Times of Loneliness
(Cincinnati: Franciscan Media, 2004)

The Shattered Lantern: Rediscovering a Felt Presence of God (Cincinnati:
Franciscan Media, 2003)